— Great Themes of the Bible —

CALL:

Called to Be God's People

Kay Huggins

ABINGDON PRESS

NASHVILLE

GREAT THEMES OF THE BIBLE
Call: Called to Be God's People
By Kay Huggins

Copyright © 2004 by Abingdon Press

ISBN 0-687-03814-6

This book is printed on recycled, acid-free, and elemental-chlorine-free paper.

Manufactured in the United States of America

06 07 08 09 10 11 12 13—10 9 8 7 6 5 4 3 2

Table of Contents

Welcome to
Great Themes of the Bible

We are pleased that you have chosen Great Themes of the Bible for your small-group study. This series of study books cultivates faith formation in contemporary life using reliable principles of Christian education to explore major themes of the Bible, the issues and questions generated by these themes, and how the Bible illuminates our response to them in daily life. The sessions provide many opportunities for spiritual growth through worship, study, reflection, and interaction with other participants.

Great Themes of the Bible Cultivates Faith Formation in Contemporary Life

Who is God? How is God at work in our world? How does God call us and relate to us? How do we relate to God and to one another? What does Jesus Christ reveal to us about God? What is the potential for life in which we choose to be committed to God through Jesus Christ? How do we find hope? Such questions are at the heart of faith formation in contemporary life.

The Bible presents great themes that are universally relevant for the faith formation of all human beings in all times and places. Great themes like call, creation, covenant, Christ, commitment, and community provide points of encounter between contemporary life and the times, places, and people in the Bible. As we reflect upon faith issues in our daily lives, we can engage biblical themes in order to learn more about God and in order to understand and interpret what it means to live with faith in God.

The great themes of the Bible are the great themes of life. They generate questions and issues today just as they did for those in the biblical world. As we identify and explore these themes, we also engage the related questions and issues as they emerge in our contemporary life and culture. Exploring the Bible helps us see how people in the biblical world dealt with the issues and questions generated by a particular theme. Sometimes they responded exactly the way we would

4

respond. Other times, they responded quite differently than we would respond. In every case, however, we can glimpse God at work as we compare and contrast their situations with our own.

In Christian faith formation, we delve again and again into the Bible as we reflect upon our daily lives in light of Christian teaching. One way to imagine this process is by envisioning a spiral. A theme in the Bible generates questions and issues. We reflect upon the theme and consider the questions and issues it raises in our contemporary lives. We read the Bible and ask ourselves how the stories and teachings inform the theme and its questions and issues. We reflect upon the insights we have gained and perhaps make adjustments in our lives. We spiral through a particular theme and its issues and questions more than once as we look to the Bible for help, guidance, and hope. As we participate in this ongoing process, we gain deeper awareness of who God is and what God wants us to do, to be, and to become. The books in the Great Themes of the Bible series are structured around this spiraling process of faith formation.

Theme

Bible

Issues and questions in contemporary life

Great Themes of the Bible Is Built Upon Reliable Christian Education Principles

The sessions in each of the books in *Great Themes Of The Bible* are based on the Scriptures and lesson guides in the *Uniform Series of International Bible Lessons for Christian Teaching.* These guides provide reliable Christian education principles to those who write the books. Session development for a book in *Great Themes of the Bible* is guided by a unifying principle that illuminates the unity between life and the Bible by emphasizing a key theme. The principle contains three components: a life statement, a life question, and a biblical response.

The lesson guides in the Uniform Series also include statements for every Scripture that help the writer to think about and develop the sessions. These statements occur in five categories or matrices: Learner, Scripture, Faith Interaction, Teaching Strategies, and Special Interest.

Statements in the Learner matrix identify general characteristics describing life stages developmental issues and particular experiences (special needs, concerns, or celebrations) that characterize learners.

Statements in the Scripture matrix identify a variety of key issues, questions, practices, and affirmations raised from the biblical texts. These may include historical, cultural, ethical, and theological perspectives.

Statements in the Faith Interaction matrix identify ways in which learners and Scripture might interact in the context of the Bible study. The statements relate to personal, communal, and societal expressions of faith.

Statements in the Teaching Strategies matrix suggest ways for writers to create sessions that connect Scripture and learners through a variety of educational methods that take into account the different ways people learn.

Statements in the Special Interest Matrix identify ways writers might address topics of special concern that are particularly appropriate to the Scripture text: handicapping conditions, racial and ethnic issues, drug and alcohol abuse, and ecology, for example. While the faith interaction matrix provides the beginning point for each session in a book in the *Great Themes of the Bible,* learning goals employed by the writers arise from all these matrices.

Great Themes of the Bible Provides Opportunities for Spiritual Growth

The books in *Great Themes of The Bible* offer you an opportunity to see the vital connection between daily life and the Bible. Every session begins and ends with worship in order to help you experience God's presence as you participate in the sessions. The small group sessions also provide opportunities to develop friendships with others that are based upon respect, trust, and mutual encouragement in faith formation.

WELCOME TO *GREAT THEMES OF THE BIBLE*

The following principles guide our approach to spiritual growth and faith formation:

- Faith and life belong together. We seek to discover connections or crossing points between what God reveals in the Bible and the needs, choices, and celebrations of our ordinary experience. Biblical themes provide this crossing point.
- Everyone is a theologian. *Theology* may be defined as "loving God with our minds" as well as with our hearts. All in your group, regardless of background, are fully qualified to do that.
- Adults learn best through reflection on experience. No longer are we blank tablets on which new knowledge must be imprinted. We can draw on a fund of experience and ask what it means for us in light of Scripture and Christian teaching about God and creation.
- Questions stimulate spiritual growth more than answers. An authoritative answer seems final and discourages further thinking, while a stimulating question invites further creative exploration and dialogue.
- Learning involves change, choice, and pain. If we are to take seriously what God is telling us in Scripture, we must be open to changing our opinions, making new lifestyle choices, and experiencing the pain of letting go of the old and moving into a new and unknown future, following the God of continuing creation.
- Community sharing fosters spiritual growth. When a group commits to struggling together with questions of faith and life, they share personal experiences, challenge assumptions, deepen relationships, and pray. God's Spirit is present. The God of continuing creation is at work.

We pray that you will experience the freedom to ask questions as you explore the great themes in your life and in the Bible. We pray that you will encounter and experience the life-transforming love of God as you become part of a *Great Themes of the Bible* group. And finally, we pray that you will see yourself as a beloved human being created in the image of God and that you will grow in your love of God, self, and neighbor.

7

Using the Books in *Great Themes of the Bible*

Each book in the *Great Themes of the Bible* series has within its pages all you need to lead or to participate in a group.

At the beginning of each book you will find:

- suggestions for organizing a Great Themes of the Bible small group.
- suggestions for different ways to use the book.
- suggestions for leading a group.
- an introduction to the Great Theme of the Bible that is at the center of all the sessions.

In each of the seven sessions you will find:

- a focus statement that illuminates the particular issues and questions of the theme in contemporary life and in the Scriptures for the session.
- opening and closing worship experiences related to the focus of each session.
- concise, easy-to-use leader/learner helps placed in boxes near the main text to which they refer.
- main content rich with illustrations from contemporary life and reliable information about the Scriptures in each session.

In the Appendix you will find:

- a list of Scriptures that illuminate the biblical theme.
- information about The Committee on the Uniform Series.
- information about other Bible study resources that may interest your group.

Books in the *Great Themes of the Bible* series are designed for versatility of use in a variety of settings.

Small Groups on Sunday Morning. Sunday morning groups usually meet for 45 minutes to an hour. If your group would like to go into greater depth, you can divide the sessions and do the study for longer than seven weeks.

Weekday or Weeknight groups. We recommend 60 to 90 minutes for weekday/weeknight groups. Participants should prepare ahead by reading the content of the session and choosing one activity for deeper reflection and study. A group leader may wish to assign these activities.

A Weekend Retreat. For a weekend retreat, distribute books at least two weeks in advance. Locate and provide additional media resources and reference materials, such as hymnals, Bibles, Bible dictionaries and commentaries, and other books. If possible, have a computer with Internet capabilities on site. Tell participants to read their study books before the retreat. Begin on Friday with an evening meal or refreshments followed by gathering time and worship. Review the introduction to the theme. Do the activities in Session 1. Cover Sessions 2, 3, 4, 5, and 6 on Saturday. Develop a schedule that includes time for breaks, meals, and personal reflection of various topics and Scriptures in the sessions. Cover Session 7 on Sunday. End the retreat with closing worship on Sunday afternoon.

Individual Devotion and Reflection. While the books are designed for small-group study, they can also be beneficial for individual devotion and reflection. Use the book as a personal Bible study resource. Read the Scriptures, then read the main content of the sessions. Adapt the questions in the Leader/Learner boxes to help you reflect upon the issues related to the biblical theme. Learning with a small group of persons offers certain advantages over studying alone. In a small group, you will encounter people whose life experiences, education, opinions and ideas, personalities, skill, talents, and interests may be different from yours. Such differences can make the experience of Bible study richer and more challenging.

Organizing a *Great Themes of the Bible* Small Group

Great Themes of the Bible is an excellent resource for all people who are looking for meaning in their daily lives, who want to grow in their faith, and who want to read and reflect upon major themes in the Bible. They may be persons who are not part of a faith community who are seekers on a profound spiritual journey. They may be new Christians or new members who want to know more about Christian faith. Or they may be people who have been in church a long time but who feel a need for spiritual renewal. All such persons desire to engage more deeply with issues of faith and with the Bible in order to find meaning and hope.

Great Themes of the Bible is an excellent small-group study for those who have completed Beginnings, a program that introduces the basics of Christian faith. It is ideal for those who are not yet involved in an ongoing Bible study, such as *Adult Bible Studies,* DISCIPLE, *Genesis to Revelation,* and *Journey Through the Bible,* or for those who prefer short-term rather than long-term studies. *Great Themes of the Bible* also provides a point of entry for those who have never been involved in any kind of Bible study.

Starting a *Great Themes of the Bible* study group is an effective way to involve newcomers in the life of your local church. If you want to start a *Great Themes of the Bible* small group as part of the evangelism program in your local church, follow the steps below:

- Read through the *Great Themes of the Bible* study book. Think about the theme, the issues generated by the theme, and the Scriptures. Prepare to respond to questions that someone may ask about the study.

- Develop a list of potential participants. An ideal size for a small group is 7 to 12 people. Your list should have about twice your target number (14 to 24 people). Have your local church purchase a copy of the study book for each of the persons on your list.

- Decide on a location and time for your Great Themes of the Bible group. Of course, the details can be negotiated with those persons who accept the invitation, but you need to sound definitive and clear to prospective group members. "We will initially set Wednesday night from 7 to 9 P.M. at my house for our meeting time" will sound more attractive than "Well, I don't know either when or where we would be meeting, but I hope you will consider joining us."

• Identify someone who is willing to go with you to visit the persons on your list. Make it your goal to become acquainted with each person you visit. Tell them about *Great Themes of the Bible. Give* them a copy of the study book for this group. Even if they choose not to attend the small group at this time, they will have an opportunity to read the book on their own. Tell each person the initial meeting time and location and how many weeks the group will meet. Invite them to become part of the group. Thank them for their time.

• Publicize the new *Great Themes of the Bible* study through as many channels as are available. Announce it during worship. Print notices in the church newsletter and bulletin and on the church Web site if you have one. Use free public event notices in community newspapers. Create flyers for mailing and posting in public places.

• A few days before the session begins, give a friendly phone call or send an e-mail to thank all persons you visited for their consideration and interest. Remind them of the time and location of the first meeting.

For more detailed instructions about starting and maintaining a small group, read *How to Start and Sustain a Faith-based Small Group,* by John D. Schroeder (Abingdon, 2003).

Leading a *Great Themes of the Bible* Small Group

A group may have one leader for all the sessions, or leadership may be rotated among the participants. Leaders do not need to be experts in Bible study because the role of the leader is to facilitate discussion rather than to impart information or teach a particular content. Leader and learner use the same book and share the same commitment to read and prepare for the *Great Themes of the Bible* session each week. So what does the leader actually do?

A Leader Prepares for the Session

Pray. Ask for God's guidance as you prepare to lead the session.

Read. Read the session and its Scriptures ahead of time. Jot down questions or insights that occur during the reading. Look at the leader/learner helps in the boxes.

Think about group participants. Who are they? What life issues or questions might they have about the theme? about the Scriptures?

Prepare the learning area. Gather any needed supplies, such as sheets of newsprint, markers, paper and pencils, Bibles, hymnals, audio-visual equipment, masking tape, a Bible dictionary, Bible commentaries, a Bible atlas. If you are meeting in a classroom setting, arrange the chairs in a circle or around a table. Make sure that everyone will have a place to sit.

Prepare a worship center. Find a small table. Cover it with an attractive cloth. Place a candle in a candleholder on the center. Place matches nearby to light the candle. Place on the worship center a Bible or other items that relate to or illuminate the session focus.

Pray. Before the participants arrive, pray for each one. Ask for God's blessing on your session. Offer thanks to God for the opportunity to lead the session.

A Leader Creates a Welcoming Atmosphere

Hospitality is a spiritual discipline. A leader helps create an environment that makes others feel welcome and that helps every participant experience the freedom to ask questions and to state opinions. Such an atmosphere is based upon mutual respect.

Greet participants as they arrive. Say their names. If the group is meeting for the first time, use nametags.

Listen. As group discussion unfolds, affirm the comments and ideas of participants. Avoid the temptation to dominate conversation or "correct" the ideas of other participants.

Affirm. Thank people for telling about what they think or feel. Acknowledge their contributions to discussion in positive ways, even if you disagree with their ideas.

A Leader Facilitates Discussion

Ask questions. Use the questions suggested in the leader/learner helps or other questions that occurred to you as you prepared for the session. Encourage others to ask questions.

Invite silent participants to contribute ideas. If someone in the group is quiet, you might say something like: "I'm interested in what you are thinking." If they seem hesitant or shy, do not pressure them to speak. Do communicate your interest.

Gently redirect discussion when someone in the group dominates. You can do this in several ways. Remind the group as a whole that everyone's ideas are important. Invite them to respect one another and to allow others the opportunity to express their ideas. You can establish a group covenant that clarifies such respect for one another. Use structured methods such as going around the circle to allow everyone a chance to speak. Only as a last resort, speak to the person who dominates conversation after the group meeting.

Be willing to say "I don't know." A leader is also a learner. You are not "teaching" a certain content to a group of "students." Instead, you are helping others and yourself to engage the great themes of the Bible as points of crossing to contemporary life and faith formation.

Introducing the Great Theme

CALL

CALLED TO BE GOD'S PEOPLE

Have you ever felt drawn into an idea, project, person, or a search? Have you encountered something so irresistible you could not turn away? Did you ever think to name that experience "a call" and wonder if God were somewhere behind or beside, under, or in that experience? In the language of faith, call signifies a particular experience. It is the connection between God and a particular individual that reveals something specific, something utterly tangible, amazingly concrete, and completely fitting for the individual to do or be. The experience of God's call is neither abstract nor general; it is precise and person specific!

That is why, although this book is titled *Called to Be God's People*, you provide much of the content of the following pages. As you read and share ideas, issues, and questions with Christian friends, each person is being called, considering a call, and responding to a call in a unique manner. This one criterion—a call fits a particular person, time, and setting—provides immediacy to the call of God. Who knows your experience of God better than you? Who has heard what you have heard calling in the night? Who knows why your heart is drawn sideways or your soul is restless or your mind continually returning to one idea? Divine calls are personal and you are the person best able to know your call. Therefore, this study begins with you and your experience.

This book also is about God's people as a collective whole, as the body of Christ. The faith of the church gathers generations of Christians who responded to God's call in Jesus Christ. Their witness gives insight into distinguishing God's call from the multitude of calling voices in our world. Stop for a moment and think about the "calls" around you:

- Calls from marketing: Buy this and you will be that.
- Calls from friends: Never turn your back on a friend.
- Calls toward success: Go to college, get a great job, live well.
- Calls of body image: Diet, body building. Look young at all costs.
- Calls of culture: Every American is 100 percent free and happy in the pursuit of happiness.
- Calls from family: You are a part of this family.
- Calls of self-fulfillment: "I wanna be me!"

As you imagine other sources of call, this list grows more complex. Sorting these calls—some loudly voiced and others subtly manipulated— is a difficult task and requires something more than one's personal experience. All around us are reliable witnesses who are able to share wisdom. The call of God may be uniquely personal, but it also occurs within a community. The church of Jesus Christ has spent centuries discerning God's call. The church's corporate witness provides invaluable models and methods for spiritual discernment. We will use the resources of our Christian tradition as we sort through the many calls in our daily lives to discover God's call.

And since we are Christians, we will use our book. The Bible contains a remarkable collection of stories about God's call, individual responses, and the consequences of saying yes and saying no. The stories often contain surprising dips, uphill climbs, and an occasional caution sign posted before a radical curve. Yet these are holy stories: stories that give meaning to our lives and transform us into more than we dream or imagine.

For this study, the Bible stories come from both the Old Testament and the New Testament. The characters we consider are well known (Abraham and Jesus) and barely known (a girl who is a slave and an old priest). Yet each plays a role in the dynamic conversation between God and humanity. All hear or help another hear God's call.

On the following pages, we will look at call from three perspectives

- Call as a relationship initiated by God, the divine intention toward reconciliation. The first two sessions pose the questions, why does God call leaders and followers and what forms does God use to call an individual? These two sessions are the foundation that allows a particular call to be discerned and developed.
- Call as participation in a task, the particular type of mission Jesus called into existence. There are three sessions relating to Jesus and his disciples. The pattern is universal in our faith. First, Jesus calls believers into an intimate relationship. Then, Jesus offers them particular ministries in full knowledge that God has blessed them with the skills, courage, and faith necessary to conduct those ministries. Finally, Jesus discloses the height and depth as well as the length and breath of discipleship. Disciples, both ancient and contemporary, learn to know God, to serve the world, and to love one another as Christ loved them.
- Call as an invitation to wholeness. This call includes you, your resistance, your response, and your transforming experience of call. The final two sessions circle around resistance and response. Again there are questions. If God's call is particular to me, why do I have difficulty hearing and responding? If I respond to God's call will I stop being me? Am I someone completely different if I say yes to God?

As you study with Christian friends, respect one another, honor God's call within your gathering, and prepare yourself to hear God's call as only you can hear. In doing so, you will exemplify the title of this book: "Called to be God's People."

Call: Called to Be God's People

Session 1

A CALL TO LEAD AND A CALL TO FOLLOW

*Genesis 11:27-12:9; 1 Samuel 16:1-4b, 6-13;
2 Samuel 7:8-16*

This session explores the surprising resourcefulness of the God who calls leaders and followers. Around this center dance other concerns about God's faithfulness, humans' fitness, and the personal question: How is God calling me?

GATHERING

Open with a quick round of "Two Truths and One Lie." Tell one another two statements of truth and one lie about jobs held, unusual volunteer work, secret ambitions realized or fantasized, for example. Try to guess which statement is the lie.

Conclude with the following prayer: "For work begun and accomplished, for calls enriching life, for dreams and visions of what could be, we give thanks to you, our God, for work, inspiration, and life. Amen."

A Call to Lead the Followers

Have you ever noticed how quickly people sort themselves into the category of leader or follower? Usually, there is little doubt about who is who. Leaders stand out by their obvious gifts, energy, courage, and imagination, while a sure-footed gait and forward-looking eyes characterize followers. It is almost as if people come with a bar code designating "Leader" or "Follower." Nonetheless, God calls leaders and followers through a myriad of ways with a simple invitation: Come, share my life.

Under close examination, the spiritual space allotted to leaders is attractive only to those thus called; followers find the lay of this land troublesome. For example, since the purpose of a leader is to direct the followers from now to then, from here to there, from so-so (or bad or worse) to good (or better or best), a leader must be willing to relocate emotionally, spiritually, and sometimes, geographically. Naturally, such relocation affects family and friends.

When a leader adds followers to life's equation, someone else—a parent, child, spouse, best friend, distant uncle, dear cousin, trusted neighbor—experiences a little loss. Leaders frequently sacrifice personal relationships for the good of the larger community and often ponder this painful oddity in their lives.

For an Extended Session
Locate a video or DVD of the movie It's A Wonderful Life. *Watch the movie together. Identify the issues of leadership demonstrated in the movie. What connections do you see between these issues and God's call?*

Jimmy Stewart confronts the terrain of leadership in the classic movie *It's A Wonderful Life.* In that story, Stewart's character, George Bailey, faces many risks, endures great personal sacrifice and tastes success only fleetingly. In fact, life is going so badly George Bailey imagines the world would be better if he never existed. His guardian angel, Clarence, proceeds to show him a world bereft of George Bailey. The harsh and ugly reality of this world shocks George out of despair. He reassesses his personal sacrifices and the broader benefits of his leadership; he chooses to return to his role of leader in family and community.

Spiritual leaders know, at soul level, that God is the source of their leadership. Their touchstone is a sense of call. Most leaders eagerly share their initial and ongoing sense of call. These tales vary in content and style, but a certain firmness—a confidence in God—is common.

> *Name a leader you respect. What would your church, organization, work site, or school look like today if that leader never lived? What does this way of thinking say about your own contribution as a leader?*

In serving others, leaders serve God. They face difficult tasks and unknown ventures confident of God's faithfulness. There are, of course, seasons of questions and discouragement; George Bailey's discouragement was not exceptional. However, leaders who respond to God's call learn to rely on God to reveal the direction, supply the skills, inspire the words, provide the renewal, and triumph despite all odds. Learning that God is trustworthy is the spiritual curriculum of Christian leadership.

A Call to Follow the Leader

The vast majority of the population, secular and religious, prefers the role of follower to that of leader. Perhaps this is so because most people assume that leaders are supposed to bear all the burdens, risks and dangers of the community, company or institution. However, since God calls followers as well as leaders, there are spiritual challenges specific to followers. Followers are neither "uncalled" leaders nor sheep trudging unthinkingly after a shepherd. Nothing is accidental; with a loving resourcefulness, God calls some Christians to lead and many others to follow.

> *Name a follower you respect. How would your world be different if that person had never lived? How would you be different? Does this change your thinking about followers or your contribution as a follower?*

Followers expand God's ways in the world; visionaries preach great sermons, but congregational members bring the good news to family, friends, neighbors, coworkers, students, teachers, strangers, and checkout clerks.

Followers widen the pathways to God. Church leaders do not invite every new resident in every neighborhood to worship; neighbors do.

Followers engage in deeds of justice and compassion. Leaders encircle the community with vision, but followers touch those who mourn, suffer injustice, fight addiction, and yearn for friendship.

Followers recognize God's presence in the everyday world. Leaders are often caught up in abstractions and dreams; followers supply hard-nosed reality.

Followers can help keep leaders on track. Followers who cherish God's future provide a standard for leaders' self-assessment.

Together, leaders and followers cooperate with God in the salvation and reconciliation of the world. The word *economy*, when applied to God, relates to the harmonious balance of redemption. In God's economy, there are sufficient resources—time, energy, and personnel—to reconcile creation. When we doubt God's economy, we side with the skeptics who hold that the world is beyond redemption.

As Christians, we trust that God, though divine economy, works for good in the world. Responsive, courageous, compassionate, and steadfast Christian leaders and followers choose to work with God in the reconciliation of the world as they respond to God's call. When in response to God's call, leaders lead and followers follow. Then the world is drawn closer together and to God.

Turning the Table

Mr. Jordan stood up to speak at a church meeting. Ordinarily reserved about voicing his opinions publicly, he was deeply disappointed by the congregation's lack of involvement in a community food project. With few words, but great passion, Mr. Jordan described his "worker bee" involvement in the food project. Then he said, "Friends, what I'm saying is this: We need new leaders. I'm not that sort of person; I don't have big visions. Still, I know that's what we need." Finished, Mr. Jordan sat down; he had no more to say.

Sally, another church member, took his words to heart. She remembered that her friend Doris once helped with food deliveries. Maybe she could find ways to engage the congregation. Sally called Doris and invited her out for coffee.

"Doris, I've been praying about Mr. Jordan's idea of becoming involved with the community food bank. I don't know exactly why, perhaps I just wanted to prayerfully support Mr. Jordan; but as I prayed, I kept thinking of you. I remembered that you once helped with food deliveries to senior citizens. Do you have some ideas about what we might do now to help?"

Has someone asked you to consider a leadership position? Has someone encouraged you to make room for new leadership? What benefits do you experience as you respond to God's call through others to in leading? in following?

"Funny you should mention the community food bank. As a matter of fact, I do have some ideas. I've just been shy about telling others what they are. Maybe this is God's way of calling me to do something."

"Why don't we call Mr. Jordan and see what we can do? I'll help."

Neither woman experienced herself as leader or an administrator of Christ's ministry. Yet the table turned. A woman heard about a need and prayed. She thought of her friend's name as a prayer's response. She courageously spoke her heart. Her friend then had to consider whether God called her to the task of leadership.

Every week in every congregation in every nation, someone who thought their ministry consisted of showing up and faithfully supporting the church is confronted with a turning table. Followers hear God calling them to lead; leaders hear God's call to follow. In the grand imagination of God, each individual has purpose and potential; and everyone is called. Moreover, God's call is dependable—it keeps coming. Regardless of human success or failure, faithfulness or forgetfulness, wisdom or ignorance, resistance or acquiescence, God imagines a reconciled world and calls individuals to further that reconciliation. Let's examine two Old Testament calls.

Abram's Call Came Late in Life

Israel's history begins with the call of Abram, the first of the patriarchs, who is later renamed Abraham. The stories leading up to the call of Abram are rich with theology and cosmology. People of faith worked out their relationship to God through the examples of these stories: Creation, Adam and Eve, Noah, and Babel. Then God spoke in a new and very specific way: God called a 75-year-old man, who was married to a barren woman of similar age.

The end of Genesis 11 states that Abram's father, Terah, intended to relocate his family from the land of Ur to Canaan. For some unknown reason, the family settled instead in Haran, in the northwest region of Mesopotamia. We know from reading this text that:

- Abram's father planned to settle in Canaan;
- Abram and Sarai were married but childless at the time of Terah's relocation;
- Abram and Sarai made their home in Haran;
- Terah's grandson Lot traveled with the family; and
- The family settled in Haran rather than continuing travel to Canaan.

Ancestral Beginnings

The Book of Genesis provides a good demonstration of the interrelationship between cultural history and sacred history. In Genesis, the stories of the first eleven chapters contain certain traditions that appear in the writings of other cultures in the ancient Near East. The dating of these stories is extremely difficult, and many scholars prefer to use a catchall category of "primeval history."

The ancestral history of the people of Israel begins with Chapter 12, the call of Abram. Although the stories of this family (beginning with Abram and continuing through Joseph) are rich in place names, there are few official names of rulers associated with historically documented dates. However, most scholars place Abram's call within Middle to Late Bronze Ages (circa 2000–1200 b.c.).

Although Biblical time measurements are often symbolic rather than actual, the family resided in Haran for a long time during which Terah lived to be an old man. Eventually, he died in Haran.

The story of Abram opens with a command, a promise, and a response. God's call to Abram was specific, "Now the LORD said to Abram, 'Go from your country and your kindred and your father's house to the land that I will show you. I will make of you a great nation, and I will bless you, and make your name great, so that you will be a blessing (Genesis 12:1-2). What an incredible call! Abram and Sarai had to leave family and go where

God directed without knowing where that would be. They would endure a challenging nomadic life in an unknown region. Their response to God's call held the promise that God would expand the family into a nation, but what could this mean? How could it be fulfilled in the later years of Abram and Sarai's life?

Read Genesis 11:27–12:9. What strikes you about God's call in this passage? What about this call might be difficult or challenging? Why? Imagine Sarai's response to Abram's decision to journey on. How did she respond?

In spite of such questions, Abram responded to God's call. He, his wife Sarai, his nephew Lot, all their possessions, and servants, journeyed, by stages, toward the Negeb, which is the southern boundary of the land of Canaan. Abram's obedience initiated a series of options for his family and community. We can only imagine the emotional journey of each member of the company.

Sarai was overjoyed by the birth of their son Isaac. The name *Isaac* means "laughter"; and it echoes Genesis 17:17 in which Abram "fell on his face and laughed" and Genesis 18:12 in which Sarai laughed as she listened to predictions of the birth of a son. Lot settled with his family on the plain of the Jordan (Genesis 13:8-18) and became ancestor of the Moabite and Ammonite people.

Have you a responsibility usually allotted to a younger person: a grandchild to raise, a youth group to sponsor, or a new business venture to begin? Compare your experience with Abram's late-in-life call to go to a new land. What connections do you see between the story of Abram and Sarai's response to God's call and the issues of leading and following? How are they leaders? How are they followers? How does their response speak to contemporary issues related to leading, following, and responding to the call of God?

David's Call Came in Early Life

David, the youngest of Jesse's sons, was tending his father's flocks when God sent Samuel to seek the future king of Israel. One by one, seven of the sons of Jesse passed before Samuel. God rejected each one and told Samuel "do not look on his appearance or on the height of his stature, because I have rejected him; for the Lord does not see

Consider the phrase, "the LORD looks on the heart" (1 Samuel 16:7b). Have you known a church leader that the world would consider to be unappealing or unpromising? How might you or your congregation look on the heart rather than the outward appearance of church leaders? What characteristics would demonstrate the right heart for leadership?

as mortals see; they look on the outward appearance, but the LORD looks on the heart" (1 Samuel 16:7.

According to human standards, any of the young men had sufficient strength, comeliness, and competence to be anointed king. Finally, Jesse's youngest son, David, was brought from the fields to the prophet. God told Samuel to anoint him because he was the one. Oddly, the young David had no experience of God calling him to be king over Israel. Indeed, after the prophet's anointing, David returned to the sheepfold and continued to grow up. There was, however, one change: "The spirit of the LORD came mightily upon David from that day forward" (I Samuel 16:13b).

Though briefly stated, this inward change was to be the essential character trait of King David. He became a man whose heart was mightily open to God's Spirit. God knew the shape of David's heart; God steadfastly worked to form the youngest of Jesse's sons into the most respected king of Israel.

Read David's story from 1 Samuel 16 to the end of 2 Samuel. For another perspective, read 1 Chronicles 11–29. What strikes you about David's story? What challenges you about it? What does it say to you about God's call? about leading? about following? about the nature of God?

There are obvious differences between God's call to 75-year-old Abram and to the teenager David. Abram's call was personal and direct; but Samuel, Jesse, and all David's brothers knew what was at stake long before David had a clue as to why he was called in from the fields. Abram was a mature man faithfully maintaining the family's status quo. He became a leader who relocated his entire family according to God's command. David's call came before his character was fully formed, and he grew into his call. Abram's call had immediate consequences for his family and community. David's call required years of struggles with Saul and with military campaigns against various enemies before the people acknowledged David as king.

Regardless of their ages and situations, both men lived faithful lives. Although he faltered and wondered if Sarai would bear a son, Abram believed God; and God "reckoned" (NRSV) or "counted" (KJV) his belief as righteousness (Genesis 15:6).

David learned obedience through his experiences with wars and lusts, murder and melancholy, and friends and enemies. Regardless of his circumstances, David held fast to God's guidance. Finally, years after Samuel

> "And he believed the LORD; and the LORD reckoned it to him as righteousness (Genesis 15:6). The English words trust and faith only partly describe Abram's response to God's call. In Hebrew, the word translated "believed" is âman, a root that suggests a constellation of meanings including "building up," "supporting," and "fostering" as well as "trust," "belief," and "being true." The word indicates that Abram's life actions emerged out of the center of his obedience and trust in God. In addition, the word translated "reckoned" (NRSV) or "counted" (KJV), includes the sense of "plait" or "weave." Thus, we can say that God weaves Abram's believing into righteousness.

anointed David, God revealed the full content of David's call through the prophet Nathan. David's "house" or dynasty would be established forever (2 Samuel 7:16). Although their tales are different, Abram and David were leaders who believed and followed God.

> How do you identify a call from God? What attributes help you discern whether God is the source of a particular call?

Our Faithful Response

How can we recognize and respond to God's call? Sometimes, God's call is so surprising that individuals wonder if they have heard clearly or if they are responding faithfully. If a course of action contains the potential for growth in mercy, justice, compassion, and love for God and others, then it is very likely to be a call from God. When God calls, faithful Christians respond with awe and dedication, persist in their relationship with God, and are faithful in worship and prayer. Consider your Christian role models as you read these concluding paragraphs.

When God calls, faithful Christians respond with awe and dedication. The title of the novel, *The Color Purple,* by Alice Walker, comes from the powerful moment when Celie sees a field of purple flowers and realizes that God created such a field to beg for our attention. Sometimes people, as Celie, stop everything and pay attention. Their attention to God is rewarded: They hear and feel and know God. Then filled with awe they act, obedient to God's call.

Whether gracefully carrying out a call or stumbling along, Christians persist in their relationship with God. It is easy to be with God's people when sins are small (and neatly hidden away), but only those who know God well understand the path through spiritual stumbling and failure. David knew his sins; David knew his God. David confessed all that was in his heart in order to stay in relationship to God. Perhaps that is why God continued to call and bless David. Leaders and followers who love God, in the long run, are blessed in their relationship with God.

Called Christians are steadfast in worship and prayer. Have you thought, *If people would just listen to one another, we would have fewer problems?* It is the same in our relationship with God. We need to listen. With Celie, Abram and Sarai, and David, Christians seek to return to that awesome place where a call began. Worship and prayer help us hear God's persistent, surprising, and purposeful call.

CLOSING WORSHIP

If you have access to a CD player or a small tape recorder, play something mellow and meditative. Listen quietly to the music and close with the following litany of gratitude.

One: For work begun and accomplished,
> (Silence for individual gratitude)

One: We give thanks to the Lord.
> All: God's steadfast love endures forever!

One: For calls by which life is enriched;
> (Silence for individual gratitude)

One: We give thanks to the Lord.
> All: God's steadfast love endures forever!

One: For dreams and visions of what could be,
> (Silence for individual gratitude)

One: We give thanks to the Lord.
> All: God's steadfast love endures forever!

One: We give thanks to you, the God of life and work and inspiration.
> (Silence for individual gratitude)

One: We give thanks to the Lord.
> All: God's steadfast love endures forever!

One: Let all the people say:
> All: Amen!

Session

2

GOD CALLS IN THE NIGHT AND AT MIDDAY

Matthew 1; Luke 2:22-38

In this session, we will look at some of the ways God calls us as we explore two stories from the narratives of Jesus' birth. These stories encourage us to become more aware of how God calls us through usual and unusual circumstances to guide us and to offer us hope.

GATHERING

As you gather, light a candle and consider the circumstances through which God has been present to you, has guided your life, and has called you toward a new direction. You may reflect silently or you may talk about these experiences with others in the group. Read Psalm 77:1-15. Use verse 6— I commune with my heart in the night; I meditate and search my spirit—as a refrain following each verse.

A Calling in the Night

When insomniacs gather, the conversation begins with requisite complaints and then swiftly shifts to tales of sleep inducing practices. Some of these are spiritual practices: praying from A through Z, silent recitation of Scripture, centering breathing, and the rhythmic practice of the prayer of the heart.

Once, while listening to insomniacs, I asked, "Why all the prayer at 3:00 A.M.?" A hardcore insomniac replied, "It's the holiest time there is!" His response rang true. Even I, who have only modest experience with sleepless nights, notice a strange openness of my mind and a spiritual quality to my thoughts in the wee hours of the night. Perhaps it is nothing more than a softening of ego defenses, but 3:00 A.M. does seem to be an hour for revelation.

> *Read the story of Joseph's dream in Matthew 1:18-24. Read the dream story of another Joseph in Genesis 37:5-11. What intrigues you about these dreams? How are they alike? How are they different? What, if anything, do these two dreams tell you about God's call?*

Woven through Scripture and the history of our faith is the testimony to God's use of dreams to call individuals to particular actions and daring deeds.

Many of our dreams are little more than the review of a sticky situation, the work on our desks, the house in which we once lived, a friend's trouble, or a recurrent chase scene from an old movie. Even at 3:00 A.M., "the holiest time there is," we may not recognize that God is present in our dreams. In the extreme moments or situations in our lives, we can become acutely aware of our need of God and thus more open to our dreams as a source of divine encounter. An extraordinary dream may interrupt an ordinary night and offer a meaningful encounter with God, an encounter that offers both guidance and hope.

Midday Visions

God offers guidance through midday visions as well as through dreams at night. There you are in the midst of an ordinary day—repairing the lawnmower, doing dishes, waiting for a bus—and suddenly some idea comes clear as day or a solution to a sticky problem seems so obvious you are embarrassed you failed to grasp it sooner!

Here is another way to unpack this idea of a midday vision. At midday, the sun is intense; there is no subtlety. Midday is the time for essentials, only essentials. Therefore, a midday vision is an intense understanding of what is already known. At midday, we "get it." The understanding hits your forehead as in the old V8 Tomato Juice commercials saying, "I coulda had a V8!" That is a secular version of a midday vision. the "it" in the call of God in dreams and midday visions is the call to peace, love, redemption, or justice. God's dreams lead toward God's way of life.

Attending to Dreams

Jungian analyst John A. Sanford makes these suggestions for attending to and understanding dreams. Using such a practice may open you to God in new and unexpected ways.

- *Write your dreams with as many details as possible. Do not censor. Collect all the material available to your awakened mind.*
- *Mull the dream over as you would an ordinary event that interests you.*
- *Associate the dream's elements freely and playfully. Write down whatever first comes to mind.*
- *Meditate on your dream; pray about the characters and situations in your dream. Allow space and time for God to speak through your meditation and prayers.*
- *Discuss your dream with a spiritual friend, someone you trust because of his or her own faith life and concern for you. If you lack such a spiritual friend, consider how and with whom you might begin such a relationship.*[1]

Sometimes a vision moment occurs in an ordinary gathering of people. Here is a story from a church board meeting. The mood of this meeting shifts from ordinary to funny to profound to faithful; moreover, there is a quiet sense of God's revelatory spirit hovering throughout. As you read, consider how God has used public humor to call you or your congregation into deeper trust, commitment, and faithfulness.

For three months the church board struggled to balance a ministry with the neighborhood youth and a tight budget for congregational needs; meetings were tense and stalled. Now the year was drawing to a close. For the meeting's opening devotions, the pastor read Isaiah 9:6-7: "For a child has been born for us, a son given to us; authority rests upon his shoulders; and he is named Wonderful Counselor, Mighty God, Everlasting Father, Prince of Peace." One church officer began to chuckle. The pastor heard nothing funny in the sacred words and was about to call the giggling gentleman to order, when another woman asked about the laughter.

> *Think about the situation leading up to the moment of understanding or insight. Did you at that time, or possibly later, feel God's involvement in the moment? Was this a midday vision for you? How did you respond? What does this experience help you understand about God's calling? In what ways have your dreams offered you insights or guidance? How do such dreams compare with those you explored in the Scriptures?"*

"It's our worry," announced the still chuckling man. "Here we sit, a few days before the celebration of Jesus' birth and all we do is worry, worry, worry about dollars and cents on a computer printout. Don't you get it? Jesus is our Wonderful Counselor, our Mighty God, our Everlasting Father, our Prince of Peace. Our little worries don't amount to a molehill compared to the mountains Jesus moves. Come on friends; let's have a little faith. Let's cut our gloom and get with the season."

> *In what way does the laughing church officer illustrate a midday vision? What happens when this individual begins to share his reason for laughing? What risk was he taking? What opposite result might have transpired? How does community response validate or invalidate a moment such as this? In what sense is this event a call from God?*

Suddenly, all the members of the board, including the pastor, were laughing at themselves. In an instant, by a nudge from Scripture and a holy laugh, one church board "got it"; and the "it" they got was simple: Jesus' mission will be accomplished. The rest of the meeting was light hearted: A few corners were cut, a few challenges accepted, and many smiles exchanged.

At the end of the evening, the board dismissed itself, with apologies to George Frederick Handel, by singing a rousing chorus of "For unto us a Son is given." There was a confident sense that Jesus was at work among them. Some said, "Ray's laughter was a holy moment." Others concurred, "The Spirit kicked us out of gloom and into light." Another said, "Our mission is as strong as the noonday sun." The pastor thought this must be a midday vision.

Among the Faithful at Midnight or Midday

Dreams in the night and visions at midday are two ways through which God may call humans. Both may be considered mystical experiences. Not all dreams are revelations from God nor does every sudden insight disclose God's heart. Rather, mystical experiences, whether as extraordinary dreams or as ordinary insight into Jesus' teaching, need solid, thoughtful testing.

Christians wisely share their mystical experiences with others in order to discern fidelity to Christian faith and to judge the integrity of mystical experiences. This process rests upon a paradox of faith: All mystical experiences are intensely private and Christian faith is profoundly corporate. Within this paradox a lively interplay exists: Mystical experiences focus church teachings, and church teachings focus mystical experiences.

What Joseph Heard

According to the Gospel of Matthew (and only according to this Gospel), Joseph had three decisive dreams:

• The first dream told Joseph to take Mary as his wife (1:20-21).
• The second dream sent the family into exile in Egypt (2:13).
• The final dream announced the time was right for a safe return to Nazareth (2:19-20).

These dreams are remarkably uncluttered by symbols to ponder and odd auditions to question. Divine messages in dreams chart a safe course for the Holy Family.

> *What are some unexpected events in your life that have involved a need to make a decision? How did you make your decision in this event? How do you think God was speaking to you in this unexpected event?*

An unexpected event occurred in Joseph's life, an event that required a decision. He discovered that Mary was pregnant. In Matthew 1:18-25, Joseph goes to sleep after having "planned to dismiss her quietly." The text says that he was "a righteous man and unwilling to expose her to public disgrace."

The word *righteous,* which can also be translated "just," means that Joseph was one who observed Jewish law. The Law of Moses would have required capital punishment (Deuteronomy 22:23-37). During Joseph's lifetime, the options would have been to bring Mary before a public court, which would bring humiliation, or to quietly hand her the divorce papers in front of two witnesses. Before his dream, he resolved to dismiss Mary quietly and thus save her from humiliation. Perhaps he went to bed that night wondering if God would bless his decision.

After experiencing what must have been a very heightened emotional state, Joseph's resolution quite likely gave him enough calm to go to sleep. He awoke with his course of action set in the opposite direction. What did Joseph hear to change his mind? Perhaps Joseph was moved by the words "Do not be afraid." These words in Matthew 1:20 and in the angelic announcements in Luke (1:13, 30; 2:10) are closely associated with the announcement God's salvation. Evidently, in the presence of angels, humans are fearful; but when fear is dismissed, love abounds.

Joseph went to bed with a resolution fashioned from fear. God steered Joseph in a different direction through a dream, and he arose able to love Mary and her child. God's guidance through the dream provided a right course of action through an unexpected crisis in his life.

Bearers of Hope

God called Joseph in an extraordinary way as he struggled with an important decision. Mercifully, God continues to enter our confusion, anger, and turmoil with a "way out." However, just as mercifully, God continues to be present and to offer hope through faithful people as they participate in the ordinary means of personal prayer, corporate worship, and service to others.

> *Form groups of two or three. Read Luke 2:22-38. What especially strikes you about this experience in the Temple? about Simeon? Anna? the Holy Family? Talk about the hopes that you have for the future. How do you see God in your hopes?*

The next two biblical characters, Simeon and Anna, prayed traditional prayers and kept holy days, fasts, and feasts. They lived in the expectation that soon God would send the Messiah.

The Temple was a gathering place for the pious. Simeon, a devout older man, very likely spent his days at the Temple praying, conversing, and observing the religious life of his people. Simeon longed to see the Messiah, and he also felt a deep and divine assurance that he would not die before his eyes beheld God's righteous one, the Messiah. The Gospel of Luke says that the Holy Spirit guided Simeon into the Temple and that he was there "when the parents brought in the child Jesus, to do for him what was customary under the law" (Luke 2:27). In fact, the Holy Spirit is mentioned three times in association with Simeon (verses 25-27). It is clear that Simeon's extraordinary vision of salvation is God-given.

Luke's Gospel refers to Anna as a prophet. Thus she, like Simeon, was a God-inspired person. She was an aged woman of extraordinary piety, who "never left the temple" and who spent everyday praying and fasting. A widow's life was difficult because widows who were not able to return to their fathers' households or to that of another close male relative were dependent on the alms and hospitality offered by strangers. Scriptures in both the Old and New Testaments show concern for the marginal existence of widows (Deuteronomy 14:29;10:17-18; Mark 12:38-44; Luke 7:11-17; Acts 6:1-6). Anna was a seasoned and pious widow, and she radiated God's Spirit through her widowhood. Her spiritual life of prayer and fasting polished her soul and no doubt prepared her to receive God's vision of salvation.

On the day that Joseph and Mary presented Jesus in the Temple for circumcision, both Simeon and Anna saw a couple from the countryside bringing their firstborn to the Temple. As Joseph, Mary, and Jesus approached, no heads or eyes turned in awe; this moment appeared to hold nothing exceptional. Simeon and Anna, however, saw something exceptional. Whether by the confident gait of the parents, an inner quickening of the Spirit, or a sudden splash of divine radiance, Simeon and Anna saw God's future wrapped as a baby boy about to be circumcised.

What they saw, they each declared. First, Simeon praised God that he was granted his heart's desire to see the Messiah. Then Anna immediately began to announce that in this baby was the redemption of Jerusalem. According to these two, the world was no longer ordinary because God's Messiah was right there in the arms of his parents, in the center of the Temple, before all who could see.

Mysteriously, by their devotion, these two old ones saw God's future in the face of an infant named Jesus. God's call through the extraordinary vision of Simeon and Anna is the call to hope.

Pay Attention

As the result of a dream, Joseph obeyed God's guidance through a difficult and unexpected event. Anna and Simeon offered hope through the God-given vision of the Messiah. All three responded to God's call. These three became living examples of the benefit of attending to God's call to action and hope.

Joseph did not question the divine origin of his dream. His years of attention to God and to righteous living gave him the spiritual sensitivity to recognize God. Moreover, the Gospel of Matthew does not hesitate to affirm that God initiated Joseph's travels to secure the family.

Simeon and Anna were clear about their experience. After years of holding on to the hope in God, near the end of their lives, they were blessed with an experience of hope fulfilled. They, like Joseph, recognized God's word because throughout their lives they faithfully attended to God. Their paths of spiritual attention continue to be appropriate for contemporary believers

CLOSING WORSHIP

In silence consider your personal affirmation of God's use of dreams and visions to guide you and to offer hope in your life. Find a partner. Talk about how God calls you to action and to hope through such experiences. Pray for one another asking God to keep you on the righteous path, supported by a hopeful heart and an attentive spirit. Thank God for the dreams and for the insights you have received.

[1]From *Healing and Wholeness,* by John A. Sanford (Paulist Press, 1977); pages 151-54.

Session

3

JESUS CALLS DISCIPLES

Mark 1:14-28; 2:13-17

In Jesus, God called a new community into being. In this session, we examine two accounts of Jesus calling disciples to work with him to proclaim the good news of the reign of God. We will explore God's good news in Jesus, the relevance of God's good news for contemporary life, and how we are called to live God's good news in our world.

GATHERING

Read Mark 1: 14-15. Use the following paraphrase from *The Message* to write a prayer inviting God's Spirit to guide your time together. "Time's up! God's kingdom is here. Change your life and believe the Message." Read your prayer to the group.

What's So Good About Jesus' Call?

Many people in Jesus' day were full of expectation for God to intervene, shake up, and bless the world with justice and peace. In our day, few people expect a divine upset, and yet the hunger for justice and peace persists. To those who listened, Jesus announced that the right time for God's action had come.

> *Form four groups. Assign the following statements from Jesus' call in Mark 1:14 to each of the four groups: Group 1: The time is fulfilled. Group 2: The kingdom of God has come near. Group 3: Repent. Group 4: Believe in the good news. What does the statement assigned to your group suggest to you? What ideas, thoughts, or feelings come to mind when you hear it? In what way can the statement speak to contemporary life?*

Jesus continues to speak a similar message to contemporary believers. The right time is now; as you hear Jesus call, God's reign surrounds; but how is that possible when the evening news is filled with terrorism and war, when the unemployment rate bounces up and down, when youth and children suffer from the abuse of drugs, and when the elderly are forgotten and left to die lonely deaths?

How does the kingdom of God come near as we work, pay the mortgage, worry about our aging parents, or try to make sense of a broken world in which war and oppression are very real? If there is something good in Jesus' call, then it must be good enough to address these and other difficult issues in our world. The good in Jesus' call is discovered in men and women who, like his original disciples, hear his invitation, turn their lives toward his ministry, and follow him.

The good in Jesus' call begins right now with us, our friends, our real life joys and concerns, and our world as we heed the call to "turn again" (repent) to God, to live God's way (kingdom), and explore what it means to be in community with other Christians.

What's the Good in This Good News?

The Gospel of Mark opens with a burst of energy. People from all walks of life, conditions, and ages flocked to be near him. Jesus' attractiveness was magnetic:

He brought God near as he exorcized demons, healed the sick, proclaimed the kingdom of God, and called people into repentance. Jesus was clear about what he was doing. In Galilee he proclaimed, "The time is fulfilled and the kingdom of God has come near; repent, and believe in the good news" (Mark 1:15). What, exactly, was this good news for those who originally heard it?

Jesus' testimony—that the time is fulfilled and the kingdom of God has come near—connected with the deepest hope of his original audience. Many of them believed that soon God would send a special emissary, a warrior-king who

Several of the prophets sowed the seeds of thought that later developed into the messianic hope that existed in the time of Jesus. For centuries, Christians have looked at several of Isaiah's thoughts as a way to understand Jesus.

- *The wolf shall live with the lamb, the leopard with the kid, the calf and the lion and the fatling together, and a little child shall lead them (Isaiah 11:6).*
- *God will destroy . . . the shroud that is cast over all peoples . . . (God) will swallow up death forever (Isaiah 25:7).*
- *The Lord will ordain peace for us (Isaiah 26:12).*
- *Then the eyes of the blind shall be opened, and the ears of the deaf unstopped; then the lame shall leap like a deer and the tongue of the speechless sing for joy (Isaiah 35:5-6a).*
- *I will pour my spirit upon your descendants, and my blessing on your offspring (Isaiah 44:3b).*
- *[God] has sent me to bring good news to the oppressed, to bind up the brokenhearted, to proclaim liberty to the captives and release to the prisoners; to proclaim the year of the Lord's favor (Isaiah 61:1).*

would defeat the Romans and reestablish the kingdom of God. Then everyone would live in freedom, peace, and full dignity as God's beloved son or daughter. When the time was fulfilled and the kingdom of God drew near, God would send a messiah. Then the hope of Israel would become a reality of everyday life.

Many believed God's messiah would initiate a time to match the prophetic picture of creation as perfectly just, peaceful, and joyful. In this new era, peace would conquer fear and blessings would

In what ways are the hopes of contemporary people similar to or different from the hopes of first-century people? Thumb through a few newspapers or magazines selecting photos that call out for God's reign of justice and peace. Discuss these pictures, and ask: What is missing? What is needed? Where is the hope? Where is the good news?

overwhelm poverty. No longer would villagers be terrorized by wild animals. No longer would people suffer illness, infirmity, and death. No longer would foreign powers inflict warfare, bondage, and domination.

In the words, actions, personality, and presence of Jesus some glimpsed these changes. It was especially the poor, the hopeless, the outcast and the dying who connected the hope of the messianic age with Jesus of Nazareth. Through him, they glimpsed the glory of God and as they drew near to him; they experienced the kingdom of God.

First, Build a Relationship

Jesus knew from the beginning of his ministry that his work required a community. Therefore, he specifically called some to be with him. His approach was direct. He observed a few men at their labors, approached them with an open greeting, and invited them to come with him as his disciples. Jesus did not invite everyone in the crowd to join him; indeed, he invited only a few, a dozen or so. As he called, he did not state his whole purpose but said, "Follow me and I will make you fish for people." With these enigmatic words, he recruited a few fishermen to become his first disciples. His first task was to build a new kind of relationship, a relationship able to carry the good news of God's salvation.

How often have you heard of a teacher recruiting students? In our contemporary world, students compete for good teachers. There is a great push to get into the best school, the most progressive training program, the advanced art course, and the master music class. In some regions of our nation, this push begins with an extensive application for preschool and is completed by interviews of three- and four-year-olds.

We are accustomed to seeking out the best teachers for subject matters as diverse as mathematics, spiritual growth, or physical fitness. In first-century Palestine, young men who wanted to study Torah listened to rabbi after rabbi before attaching themselves to one as disciples. Rabbis did not search for students and rabbis certainly did not call students as followers. However, Jesus called his disciples. He did so purposefully; he was preparing for the future.

Jesus Called Working People

In the television dramas and on the big screen, Jesus' intense stare convinces working fishermen to drop their nets and walk away with him. It is a romanticized image. Jesus initiated the relationship with the disciples by calling them. First, however, he observed their work habits, noticed their personal relationships, watched them put shoulder to the task, and recognized their work relationships.

Before Jesus approached the fishermen, he knew quite a bit about them. One thing did not escape his attention: These men were born to be fishermen. Jesus also knew their culture. If they had

Read Mark 1:16-22. What qualities do you think Jesus identified as he watched the fishermen doing their work? Use your imagination to be as specific as possible. How might these qualities or skills be useful in Jesus' ministry? What qualities do you observe among your workmates or colleagues? How might these be useful in Christian ministry?

not responded to the call of Jesus, these men would most likely die as fishermen. However, Jesus saw more than nets and fish and the sea in these fishermen's future. He saw their potential as coworkers in proclaiming the good news of God's kingdom way of life.

What the Fishermen Knew

Feeling the positive evaluation of Jesus surely drew the fishermen toward him. It is likely, however, the fishermen knew something about Jesus as well. An itinerant preacher announcing God's season of salvation was certainly news among the villages of Galilee. Word spread swiftly, even when carried by those who traveled on foot. Moreover, these men probably observed Jesus as he watched them.

Although the Gospel of Mark uses the word *immediately* to describe their change from the old life of fishing to the new life with Jesus,

> *What do you see as the consequences of the fishermen leaving their nets to follow Jesus? What do you see as the benefits? Read Mark 1:14-28 again. Why do you think they chose to follow Jesus?*

God's own quiet preparation probably assisted with the transition. After all, the change was huge. The fishermen's decision to go with Jesus very likely provoked economic strain within the fishing community, emotional turmoil for close friends and loved ones, cultural instability by the challenge to fixed vocational assumptions, and an uncertain future of traveling on the open road with Jesus.

Romanticism sees the rosy side of the decision to leave; realism sees another side. The truth of the experience was probably somewhere in between. When the fishermen immediately left their nets, the whole town experienced loss and confusion; yet their action ultimately ignited hope and illuminated God's redemption. The call of the fishermen happened on one day, but its impact began before and continues beyond that one day.

An Outsider Comes In

Outsiders are those who by others' assumptions, prejudice, or blind spots are excluded from full participation in culture or institutions such as the church. Mark 2:13-17 provides an example of just such an outsider

> *When you hear the term* outsider, *who or what group in our contemporary culture comes to mind? Who are the people deemed unacceptable? Read Mark 2:13-17 again. What does it say to you about the new community God is calling together?*

during the time of Jesus, an outsider called by Jesus. Jesus called Levi, a tax collector, and as he joined with Levi's friends—persons assumed to be of no regard—Jesus confronted a deep prejudice.

Tax collectors were officially outsiders in Israel who were excluded from social and religious settings because of their choice of vocation. Collecting taxes was an outrageous choice because everyone knew that cheating was the name of the tax collecting game.

Rome did not issue tax schedules or standards. Instead each province was informed of the total amount of tax to be remitted to Rome. Tax collectors were expected to create their salary by adding it to the amount due to Rome, thus creating opportunity for fraud and extortion. The tax system was built on deception and greed. All tax collectors were assumed to be crooks who were willing to cheat the wealthy and the poor in order to line their own pocketbooks. They were also seen as traitors to their own people because they worked for Rome. Because of their contact with Gentiles, they were considered to be ritually unclean, which excluded them from religious practice in the Temple.

Jesus continually bumped up against the assumptions and prejudices of his culture. Being a Galilean, Jesus knew prejudice firsthand. In John 1:45-46, when Phillip tells Nathaniel about Jesus, son of Joseph of Nazareth, Nathaniel replies, "Can anything good come out of Nazareth?" Frequently, Jesus intentionally crossed boundary lines to bring his greeting, peace, healing, and friendship to people clearly labeled outsiders.

Bringing an outsider into the circle of followers was a prophetic and a costly action. Dining at his house with a roomful of sinners (that is, outsiders) was outrageous. Such actions, however, were but tiny indications of the length to which Jesus would go to share God's love with those who needed it most. He called the outcast, healed the sick, forgave the sinners, and loved the unloved. Deeds like these are dangerous; eventually, someone will pay when cultural assumptions and prejudices are challenged as illegitimate. Jesus not only shared his life with his friends, he gave it away relationship by relationship. Ultimately, he gave his whole life for the world he loved.

Called Into Christ's Community

The church of Jesus is composed of all persons Jesus has called to be his own. This includes women and men, the young and the ancient, scholars and nonreaders, the chic and the street smart. All who hear Christ's call and turn to him in faith are welcome in the Christian community. Or so we say. In actual practice, we are more like those in the time of Jesus who struggled to understand why Jesus associated with the outsiders, the unacceptable people. We are uncomfortable with the knowledge that Christian communities are called to invite the outsiders or the unacceptable" into the family. The church should be a place where people relate to one another as Jesus related to people; yet, all too often, the reverse is true as in the following story:

After a keynote address to a large ecumenical gathering, the speaker remained near the dais to greet the audience. Her speech had included a strong call for all denominations to extend their reach into contemporary culture and become more inclusive. An older African American woman slowly made her way toward the speaker. "I understand what you mean about reaching out in our towns and communities . . . I'm not objecting to that; but I have to tell you," the woman paused gathering courage to challenge the guest. "I have to tell you that for most of my life, I've not felt included in my church. Don't you think God is getting tired of some folks pretending others folks don't exist? I'm tired of being an outsider inside my church." The speaker fumbled for words then slowly extended her hand and said, "Yes, and I'm tired with you."

> *How does your congregation invite, welcome and build relationships with new believers? Is there a specific program for evangelism or does every member undertake this task? How did you become involved in your current congregation? Have you invited others to visit your congregation?*

As the disciples were called to be with Jesus in order to reach out to others with the good news of God's kingdom, so contemporary Christians also are called into relationship with Jesus. However, the multicultured, multidenominational, multinational church of Jesus Christ is different from a small band of disciples. The disciples sat with Jesus and discussed the events of the day. They asked him to clarify his teachings. They turned to him for direct support when discouraged with their ministry failures.

Contemporary Christians are faced with the difficult task of sorting through official pronouncements of their denomination, even as they hear tales of the standards of other denominations. When a contemporary Christian searches the Internet for something as familiar as John 3:16, a half a million hits turn up. The yellow pages offer a number of listings for "Christian counselors." The sea of Christian resources swells to overwhelming. However, this amazing and somewhat unwieldy contemporary body of Christ still calls men and women, one by one, into Christian community. The contemporary church continues to use Jesus' model of community.

- Begin with a relationship. Introduce Jesus and his friends to newcomers.
- Grow by intention. Honor and nurture everyone's potential.
- Mature steadfastly by listening for Jesus' call to accompany him into the world.

Indeed, Jesus' call creates something wonderful in the world: communities of people related to each other through Jesus and ministries where the world can be loved to wholeness.

CLOSING WORSHIP

Spend a few moments prayerfully thinking about the qualities and skills for ministry among the people in your group. What qualities do you see? What skills are admirable? How are these qualities and skills a part of the ministry of your congregation? Consider your own skills and talents. In what specific ways can you offer the talent or skill to your local congregation? your community? How might you adjust behaviors and perceptions to improve relationships in your life? How might you recognize and accept the outsider (or yourself) as accepted by God? Offer thanks to God for any insights you gain and for new commitments you make in response to God's call.

After this time of silent prayer, tell another group member about the qualities and skills for ministry that you observe in them. Thank this person for responding to Jesus' call. After the affirmations are shared, close with the following prayer: "God, you give your people abundant gifts for ministry; grant that we may appreciate all your gifts, remember their purpose, and effectively use them to share good news in our world. Thank you for Jesus' persistent call to those within and outside circles of acceptance. May we ever expand his love in our lives, families, church, community, nation, and world. Amen."

Session 4

JESUS SENDS AND EQUIPS DISCIPLES

Mark 3:13-19; 6:6b-13

In this session, we dig into the mission to which Jesus called and equipped his disciples. In addition to an intimate relationship with our Lord, Jesus calls men and women into a new way of living that is characterized by generosity, compassion, and trust. This new way of living is directed toward others – especially toward those most in need of God. The name of this new way of living is ministry.

GATHERING

Read the focus statement. List the ways your church demonstrates generosity, compassion, and trust. List the ministries that are directed toward those most in need of God. List the ministries that reach outside the church to those who are not yet involved in the life of the congregation. Conclude with a prayer of gratitude for the specific projects or individuals in your congregation's witness. Ask for God's help as you consider ways God in Christ calls and equips people to share Christ's love with a hurting world.

What's Expected of Me?

What's expected of me? It is a good and a frequently posed question as youth and adults consider joining a church. Just as frequently as it is posed, the response comes: "Not too much." Then, a list checks off the obvious: regular attendance at worship (when you can make it, that is), financial support of the budget (as you are able, that is), involvement in a class to help you grow wise in your faith (if you want to grow, that is), some engagement in a project that serves others (we will talk about that later).

Consider these anecdotes gleaned from two very different settings for ministry. In each, a ministry is initiated through the call of one individual to do something faith-filled.

The Honey Tithe: In a country congregation, a man who was a beekeeper quietly presented his "honey tithe" to the church each year. The children, inspired by his simple practice of generosity, began their own campaigns to earn and tithe money. Soon the whole congregation was contributing to the honey tithe, and the church council was discovering new ways to respond to exceptional community needs.

Form two groups. Group 1 will read "The Honey Tithe," and Group 2 will read "A Church Basement." Discuss how each is a response to Jesus' call to ministry, the spiritual graces necessary for each ministry, and similar ministry stories from your congregation or past experience. Tell the entire group about your discussions. How might you, as an individual, a group, or a congregation, expand your response to Jesus' call to serve others?

A Church Basement: At a large, aging, and minimally maintained urban church facility, the janitor was the person most knowledgeable about the building. He was also a seasoned saint and saw potential where others could not. Through his clear witness, the congregation turned the corner on their discouragement about the shabbiness of their aging facility and initiated a new ministry for community youth. Although the context was personal, the outcome served many.

The janitor's grandson lived in the neighborhood of the church; as he entered his teen years there was less and less supervision of the child. Worried that his grandson could easily drift into trouble, the janitor approached the pastor with an idea. He offered to invite his grandson and a few of his friends to work with him on repairing the basement. He knew the congregation could not afford to pay the youth, but he wondered if some space in the basement could be theirs. The pastor considered the idea; the church council was cautious, yet permitted the project.

The janitor's invitation to his grandson included the boy's friends. That fall, a group of five to seven youth gathered several times a week to remove peeling paint, crumbling plaster, and splintering wood. Within months, they turned the basement into a bright and inviting space. The pastor was pleased, the church council approved, and the janitor was relieved. Then they dreamed on.

The congregation proposed a partnership with the neighborhood junior high school, an after-school program to teach young people practical skills, as well as art, music, and drama. Eventually, a grant brought seed money to establish a center for young teens. The congregation, through the inspiration of their janitor, grew in their awareness of the challenges and hopes for youth in their community. At the beginning of this story, no one guessed what might eventually evolve.

The School of the Church

The disciples had their relationship and travels with Jesus; we have the school of the church. They had hot dusty roads, nights dependent on hospitality, and demanding, needy crowds. We have air-conditioned buildings, some minor difficulties with the parking lot, and a few significant challenges to love the unlovable. How-ever, in both settings, then and

What is the curriculum in your school of the church? What specific opportunities exist in which you might participate and thus learn more about how your own call from Jesus? Who are the teachers? Who are the students? What do you anticipate next for your congregation's ministry? What will your role or task be? How have you participated in ministry? What are the roles of clergy, staff, and members in Jesus' contemporary mission in the world?

now, the call of God is the invitation to stay close to Jesus and in relationship with his people. As we do that, something amazing happens: Each learns the particulars of his or her call.

In truth, there is no template of Christ's call; there is, rather, the invitation to "come and see" (John 1:39). It is as we enroll in the school of the church that God's initial call can become personally clear and focused. Interestingly, in this school, we are invited to learn by doing.

Most congregations actively promote ways to be involved in ministry because most congregations know that such engagement stretches faith, provokes deeps questions, and results in bold witness to Christ's compassion for the world. Such involvement may be as simple as recording the weekly worship attendance (which may spark a whole new approach to evangelism) or as complex as organizing a community effort to restore a park overrun by drug users (which may lead to greater ecumenical unity in a community).

Every Christian is invited to take small yet necessary steps in ministry. When small tasks are accompanied by faithful reflection something amazing happens: Not only do individuals grow in faith but Christ-like ministry blesses the community and world. There is always a way to begin, but rarely does one see where the beginning will lead. This school of the church provides spiritual succor for hungry hearts and abundant blessings to a world in need.

Equipped for Discipleship

Growing in faith and helping others grow in faith takes time and commitment, as well as a few successes and a few failures. Jesus was willing to give his disciples time to experience all these in order to equip them for their discipleship. He called them; they traveled with him. He taught them; they discussed among themselves. He performed signs and wonders; they pondered the source of his power. He gave instructions; they practiced new behaviors. He took time with them; they matured into effective disciples.

If Jesus had explained all that gospel ministry demanded, the disciples (as contemporary new members) might have responded, "This is definitely too difficult." Because there was time for relationships, skills, trust, and courage to develop, Jesus' disciples changed the world.

Mark's Gospel shows the beginning of this world-changing ministry in the narratives that tell of choosing the Twelve and sending them out to do some specific tasks

Selected and Sent

Mark, in his usual terse manner, introduces the disciples as "those Jesus wanted" and states their mission was to proclaim Jesus' message and to cast out spirits. Most of what we know about these men is gleaned from scraps of information drawn from Scripture, scholarship, church history, and legend. Though we know little about their lives, we do know that their lives were transformed because they responded to Jesus' call.

> *Jesus saw in each disciple a contribution to his ministry. What does this imply for you? What methods are employed in the calling of leaders in your congregation? How might Jesus' call occur in your congregation?*

Simon (Jesus called him Peter, the rock), the most prominent disciple of Jesus was a fisherman from Galilee; his name suggests the dual culture of Jewish and Roman typical for the Diaspora. He probably spoke Aramaic and Greek. Peter's leadership fades in Acts 12. Tradition suggests his ministry concluded with martyrdom in Rome.

James and John, the Sons of Zebedee. Jesus nicknamed them "the sons of thunder." We can only guess why he did so. These Galilean fishing partners of Peter and Andrew formed the inner circle of Jesus' disciples. The record of James's martyrdom is the only scriptural account of an apostle's death (Acts 12:2). John became an important leader in the Jerusalem church after the death of his brother.

Andrew, brother of Simon Peter. According to church legend, Andrew became the patron saint of both Russia and Scotland.

Philip. Another fisherman from the Sea of Galilee. He is not Philip, the evangelist mentioned in Acts; however, by the second century, this persistent confusion had begun.

Bartholomew. Because this may not be his full name, much confusion surrounds the identity of this disciple. Church tradition described him as a missionary to various nations and countries.

Matthew. By a very early tradition, Matthew is a tax collector (some suggest he is Levi). The early church attributed the first Gospel to him. There is a tale of his peaceful death and two more of his violent death: one by fire and another by sword.

Thomas. His Hebrew/Aramaic name designates a twin. Some early Christian traditions designate him as Judas Thomas, suggesting that he is a relative of Jesus (as Thaddaeus below). Present-day Christians of Saint Thomas of India trace their faith to Thomas; however, the beginnings of this faith community are not documented.

James, the son of Alphaeus. Some early texts substitute Levi, the son of Alphaeus, for James. This James is not mentioned other than in the lists of disciples.

Thaddeus. Some scholars claim his formal name is Judas, a brother or a cousin of Jesus (Matthew 13:55). Nothing more is known. Church tradition includes a story about Judas's two grandsons who by their witness convince Emperor Domitian to end the persecution of the church. These two later became church officials.

Simon the Cananaean. Mark 3:18 contains the only reference to this disciple in the New Testament. His designation stems from an Aramaic word for "zealot"; he was probably a revolutionary. Church legends suggest that this Simon was the son of Clopas and successor of James, head of the Jerusalem church.

Judas Iscariot. The common interpretation of Judas's name is "from Kerioth" making him the only Judean among the disciples. Traditions abound regarding his personality, motivations in ministry, betrayal, and death. Scripture and church tradition agree he died a violent death, and land was purchased as a result of his betrayal of Jesus.

As you can read, there is little information about the men Jesus called. Each subsequently served the church, and most were honored, at least in church tradition, as true martyrs (the Greek word for "witness") of the Christian faith. We know so little, yet they did so much.

Provisions for the Journey

In Mark 3:13-19, Jesus affirmed his relationship with the disciples and defined two tasks of ministry as proclamation and exorcism. The conduct of ministry was more fully defined in Mark 6:6b-13 as Jesus instructed his disciples to:

- minister in pairs, rather than independently;
- depend on the hospitality of others rather than encumber themselves with provisions;
- travel with utmost modesty: limited funds, food, clothing, for example;

> *Read Mark 3:13-19 and 6:6-13 slowly and quietly. What particular words attract your attention? Why? How do these words support or challenge your understanding of ministry?*

- refrain from unnecessary movement from house to house; and
- not waste time with unwelcoming homes, families, and communities.

All these rules stressed one attitude: The disciples were to trust God's direction of their work. By practicing trust, they learned to trust. This model for ministry continues to be instructive in the contemporary church.

Stepping Out in Faith

Jesus' call to the disciples grew and matured through the addition of the tasks of ministry. As the disciples stepped out in faith, they proclaimed the gospel and they healed the hurts of many; but what is expected of contemporary disciples? Are we called to proclaim the good news? In a word, yes.

Every Christian will at some time, in some situation, to some particular individual or institution speak the word of Christ. Consider some of the many ways proclamation occurs: telling other people about Jesus, identifying and taking action against injustice in its many forms, expressing mercy or compassion with simple deeds of caring, praying for others, attending worship and other

> *What comes to your mind when you hear the words "proclaim the gospel"? What feelings do you have when you hear or read those words? What have you learned about proclaiming the gospel from other Christians? What negative images come to mind? What positive ones?*

church functions, participating in a mission trip or program, contributing time or talents to do a specific task in a local church, and giving money to support the ministry of the church.

Casting Out Spirits

List current threats to the security offered by our worldview. What happens when a world-view is questioned?

Jesus commissioned his disciples to share the good news and to cast out spirits. As contemporary disciples, we accept and use his ministerial guidance related to the first part of his commission; but we pause before the second. Are contemporary Christians called to cast out spirits? Before we make a snap judgment, let's compare our worldview with that of first-century Palestine.

We live in a world that we assume we can understand, explain, and control. Scientific discoveries bring us knowledge. Art, music, and drama offer depth of meanings. Technology yields creature comforts. We believe in good education that will nurture high ideals and enable us to minimize most difficulties in life. We put our trust for health, happiness, and comfortable living in good nutrition, affordable housing, safe means of transportation, numerous forms of communication, wise financial planning, and medical research.

The realm of the unknown appears to shrink with every scientific breakthrough. We think we understand the world, and we anticipate that in the future we will understand even more. Our trust in such knowledge, whether correctly or mistakenly so, gives us a sense of security.

In Jesus' world, the realm of the unknown was huge; moreover, every unknown bit of reality was explained as an invasion of the spirit world. While we strive to know the world as it is, they readily confessed there was more to reality than observable tangible "stuff." Jesus sent his disciples out to confront the "more" of reality and to cleanse human life of all the unknown forces resulting in bondage, fear, despair, and hopelessness. The thrust of their confrontation was love. Their energy came from the gospel announcement that God's season of favor began in Jesus. By their bold witness, the disciples broke the bonds that held many in subjection, whether the domination came from fear, physical or mental illness, or societal exclusion. Jesus' good news was powerful; even un-named forces responded to what God was doing through Jesus.

Turning from first-century Palestine back to our contemporary world, we ask, how do we challenge the spirits creating bondage, fear, despair, and hopelessness in our society? In every age, the church (and each Christian) is called to confront and cleanse the world's hurts and harms. In answer to our original question, "Are we called to cast out spirits?" Yes! We are called to exercise authority over spirits, be they spirits of prejudice, addiction, abuse, materialism, militarism, hatred, violence, impersonal science or postmodern skepticism.

Christ gives authority, skill and power to his disciples today, just as he did in Galilee. As we practice our faith by small acts of charity, generosity, compassion, and love, Christ nourishes our souls with energy and love. Gradually, we grow into a new way of living. Not only do we know and trust Jesus more, we also accomplish more for those in need. By staying close to Jesus and stepping out in ministry, God's love abounds.

CLOSING WORSHIP

Sit quietly and meditate on one of the three questions: What have you done for Christ? What are you doing for Christ? What will you do for Christ? Close with this prayer: "Christ, you call us to journey with you in the great company of those you love and call. Help us to step out in faith, reach out in compassion, and move according to grace. May our deeds of mercy and justice reveal God's reign on earth. Nurture the good deeds begun, inspire new Christian ministries and, as you have in the past, forgive us for our failures to love you, our brothers and sisters, our community, and our world. Bless our work completed, begun, and yet to be imagined. This we pray in the name of Jesus. Amen."

Session

5

CALLED TO BE MORE

Mark 8:27-38; 10:13-45

In this session, Jesus' calls his followers to total commitment and to a deeper understanding of the way of life that leads to God's vision of true greatness. The disciples misunderstood Jesus and were, understandably, resistant. Contemporary Christians share the same glimpse of God's vision in Jesus' teachings and a similar resistance. This session calls us to consider what more, in addition to personal relationship and engagement in ministry, is included in Christ's call.

GATHERING

Sing or read the hymn "Where He Leads Me." What encouragement is available through these hymns? What challenges? Read the session focus above. What does the phrase "total commitment" mean to you? Pray together: Dear God, you have called us to be disciples of Jesus. You promise to show us the way and to walk with us. Help us long to discover all that you intend for us. In Christ we pray. Amen.

Commitment is a challenging word for many people in today's world. Many feel over-committed already, and they are all too familiar with the experience of burnout. What can total commitment to the call of Jesus possibly mean to those who live every day of their lives with huge commitments of time and energy? Consider the following examples of busy people:

- working parents who must meet the demands of their careers, attend to the needs of their children, maintain a household, prepare meals, do laundry, and give time to one another
- a successful executive in the business world
- a person who must care for aging parents
- someone who must work two jobs in order to pay monthly bills
- a person who never says no when asked to do something

How can a person give what they feel they do not have? Does the call to total commitment mean placing more burdens on someone who already feels overwhelmed? The questions are not unreasonable.

Other people are frustrated by a lack of commitment in relationships, and still others feel a sense of entitlement that eliminates the notion of commitment from their thoughts. Jesus taught his disciples that God's way of life blossoms abundantly and eternally as people give total commitment to God's purposes. His words confounded first-century disciples. They continue to challenge contemporary disciples. Considering all you are and do, what more could Jesus ask of you?

Recall a TV show that you have recently watched. Evaluate the commitments to self, others, culture, and God in the show. How were commitments honored or exploited? Were there instances of sacrifice and service? Did any use "nobody's perfect" as an explanation of behavior? When have you been on the receiving end of this explanation in committed relationship or used "nobody's perfect" as your own excuse?

Nobody's Perfect

"Nobody's perfect." It seems whenever the conversation turns to the demand for a higher accountability, a thoroughly just response or a rigorous exhibition of righteousness, someone says, "Nobody's perfect." That someone may claim to be excusing others from a higher moral standard, but the phrase "Nobody's perfect" is often a smoke screen to hide the speaker's personal resistance. Confident that there will be no disagreement, the proverbial "Nobody's perfect" is deployed to halt a conversation that will demand more time, more energy, more commitment, and perhaps a more careful look at what one values. It is a smokescreen that works. We are humans by birth and God calls us to be Christians. We frequently sin and fall short of the glory of God. We demonstrate, over and over again, "nobody's perfect." It is a cunning strategy based on just enough truth to stop a discussion about Jesus' expectations of believers. After all, who is ready to argue that humans are perfect?

A New Perspective

Even as we acknowledge human frailty and imperfection, our Christian calling is a high calling. Jesus' call is an invitation to become, through the grace of God, more committed to the vision of God and a way of life that often stands on contradistinction to the ways of the world in which we live. Jesus knows our human hearts, minds, and will; yet Jesus sees our potential, our progress, and even our saintliness. As Jesus engages us, the distance between saint and sinner is bridged not by exceptional effort or obsessive introspection, but by a bold confidence in God. Jesus' call is not an either/or choice, rather it is an invitation to journey with him though life. On this journey, in spite of our imperfections, we learn to live in freedom, peace, justice, and most of all, love. This journey is based on a new perspective that silences the "nobody's perfect" excuse.

I once felt a strong outrage over the rising number of teenage parents in our culture. Instead of focusing my outrage on the economic and social circumstances that contribute to the phenomena, my outrage was turning into a prejudice toward the teenaged parents themselves.

In truth, I knew only one teenage parent intimately; and she was doing a great job of parenting her child and completing her high school education. I regretted the reign of such prejudicial thinking in my mind and heart; and I prayed about it, confessing my prejudice and asking God to help me be more sensitive to teenaged parents. I looked for every possible good; and, surprisingly, I began to see these teenaged parents and their children in a different light. The change in perspective allowed a new approach to a difficult social issue and opened my heart to a new community in which I might be more supportive in a difficult life circumstance.

Jesus taught his disciples a new perspective. He taught them to think abundantly in order to live abundantly according to the rule of God. The abundance Jesus shared with his disciples began with relationship. He called them to him in order that he might be with them. Out of that relationship, he offered them a vision of the world as secure and safe in God's care. Through specific ministry assignments, Jesus honed the disciples' trust in God. As they matured in their trust, he led them to a full commitment to God's vision for a redeemed world. It was a gradual process and one fraught with risks and temptations; still, Jesus carefully led the disciples from an initial response, into active participation in ministry and finally to total commitment and true greatness. Let's observe Jesus' strategy for discipleship as recorded in the Gospel of Mark.

Total Commitment for the Followers of Jesus

In Mark 8:27-38, Jesus emphasized the need to think again about what would happen to the Son of Man and to think again about the implications for those who were his followers. Jesus wanted his disciples to understand God's abundant love for all creation and God's vision for life in God's realm, a vision that was different from what his followers had in mind. The traveling ministry had reached the point at which they would begin the journey to Jerusalem. Here Jesus disclosed his future and began to teach the disciples about their future. He questioned his disciples. What had they heard others say about him? What were they thinking about him? As a skillful teacher with a carefully prepared instructional plan, Jesus examined their thinking and called them to consider what total commitment would mean.

Read Mark 8:27-38. What is the strongest challenge that you see in this passage? How do you see this challenge in your daily life? How do you understand Jesus' words in verses 34-35? What relationship do you see between total commitment to Jesus and setting priorities in a busy life?

64

Peter called Jesus "Messiah," a term that means "anointed." In the time of Jesus and the disciples, many believed God would send a "warrior-king" who would defeat the Romans, assume the throne, and reestablish a monarchy based on the rule of God. Jesus responded to Peter by sternly telling them not to tell anyone about him (8:30). He began to teach them that the Son of Man "must undergo great suffering, and be rejected by the elders, the chief priests, and the scribes, and be killed, and after three days rise again" (8:31).

> *What pushed or propelled you to grow spiritually? Was growth stimulated by triumph, tragedy, trials, or triumphs? Divide your lifeline into thirds; describe your concept of God in each third, significant challenges to your beliefs, and subtle or dramatic shifts in your faith.*

When Peter rebuked Jesus for challenging existing perspectives regarding the Messiah, Jesus issued his call to the disciples and to the crowds. "If any want to become my followers, let them deny themselves and take up their cross and follow me. For those who want to save their life will lose it, and those who lose their life for my sake, and for the sake of the gospel, will save it" (8:34-35). The gain for such total commitment was the life and power of the kingdom of God.

Jesus taught about following, cross-bearing, saving one's life, and losing one's life. These are lessons for the mature in faith, lessons well beyond the Christianity 101 of the first half of Jesus' teaching time with his disciples.

As a teacher, Jesus was insistent; he intended that his disciples move from a superficial idea of God's messiah to a deep, daring trust that the Son of Man would overcome suffering, evil, and death by living through all of it. As long as the teaching journey to Caesarea Philippi had been, even longer would be the teaching journey to Jerusalem. The disciples learned God's abundant love as they traveled through the northern regions of Galilee; as they headed south, they learned a trust that bears all things.

True Greatness

Heading south, Jesus and his disciples journeyed toward Jerusalem. The new teaching theme is a continuing exposition on true greatness

Form three groups. Group 1 will read Mark 10:13-16, Group 2 will read Mark 10:17-22, and Group 3 will read Mark 10:23-27. Create a definition of "true greatness" based on your passage. Gather together again as one large group. Tell about the theme of your groups passage and your definition of "true greatness." What do the definitions in the Scriptures say about our contemporary culture?

that is demonstrated by an attitude of humility, by what a person values, and by the willingness to serve others. Jesus' lessons for the disciples overflowed with content, and most of the content is difficult.

The Greek word Jesus used to explain himself is *diakoneo,* which is generally translated "to serve." It is rooted in the concept of a servant who waits on tables or an attendant who brings the food to houseguests. This role was not distinguished in the first century. In Mark 10, several characteristics of servanthood are included. In contemporary wording, these are:

- The innocent are to be honored. Because they are dependent, they teach others how to live before God (10:13-16).
- After every avenue to happiness has been tried, the one who truly seeks God must face his or her obsession with security; there is no faith without loss or risk. With God, the impossible is always possible (10:17-27).
- God remembers and blesses everyone who follows Jesus for the sake of the good news, yet personal sacrifice does not rule out suffering (10:28-30).
- There is a surprising order in God's reign. Expect an upset of ordinary standards; those assured of their importance and status, as well as those with great insecurities before others, will be surprised by God's new order (10:31).

Each teaching was demonstrated in the way that Jesus lived, and watching Jesus was a crucial part of the disciples' education. However, when Jesus spoke about his suffering and death, his words sparked the disciples' strong repudiation.

In Chapter 8, Peter rebuked Jesus after the first mention of suffering and death; in Chapter 10, James and John (members of the most trusted inner circle) requested special privileges after Jesus told them for the third time that the Son of Man would suffer, die, and rise again (Mark 8:27-33; 9:30-37; 10:33-34). It is almost as if the disciples must resist—by any and every means—this hard teaching.

Contemporary Christians from all segments of society—the poor, the working poor, middle class, and wealthy—experience a similar resistance. In our culture it is almost impossible to believe the teaching that the way to life and power is to give to God total commitment that may involve personal sacrifice and to serve rather than to be served. Yet, with God, this impossible belief is possible.

Signs of Maturing Faith

The Gospels, especially the Gospel of Mark, portray the disciples as slow to recognize the full import of Jesus' teachings for their discipleship. Mark's Gospel offers in these

> How does God's vision of a reconciled world nurture congregational ministry? the call to serve others in the name of Jesus Christ?

views of the disciples' stubborn misunderstanding points of identity for Christians like you and I who are prone to veer away from the path of commitment and true greatness. Still, miracles occur in our daily lives of faith. In our faith struggles, something in us quickens toward compassion, mercy, justice, and servanthood.

God's vision of the kingdom through Jesus consistently, persistently draws human creatures near. God's compassion sparks hearts to serve. God's longing for justice will work through the smallest of gaps in our prejudices. God's response to human culpability forgives the past and inspires new deeds worthy of our calling. Regardless of its modest

> What signs of maturing in faith do you observe in your life and among your Christian community? Select four or five marks of Christian maturity from the list. Using colored highlighters, analyze your church newsletter according to these marks. What predominates? What is implied but not directly stated? What is obvious by its absence? Share your analysis in a frank conversation about the role and responsibility of your congregation in helping disciples to mature in their faithful living.

imprint on a human soul, our response to God's vision matures when tended with love and expectation.

Often people are more aware of their failures rather than the signs of their personal development. It does Christians good to affirm their spiritual growth. The results of such evaluation are both humbling and encouraging. We are humbled as we recognize the modesty of our soulful work, but encouraged by the changes that time, prayer, and practice have developed. Here's a summary of common Christian practices, disciplines, and duties found in *Growing in the Life of Faith,* by Craig Dykstra.[1] Use a few of these to measure the maturing of the past decade.

- worshiping God together
- telling the Christian story to one another
- interpreting together the Scriptures and the history of the church's experience
- praying together and by ourselves
- confessing, forgiving, and being reconciled with one another
- tolerating one another's failures and encouraging each other
- carrying out specific tasks of service and ministry
- giving generously
- suffering with and for one another
- providing hospitality and care to friends, strangers, and even enemies
- listening and talking attentively about our faith
- struggling to become conscious of our culture and context
- criticizing and resisting powers and patterns that destroy human beings, corrode human community, and injure God's creation
- working together to maintain and create social structures that accord with God's will

The goal of our faith is maturity in Christ. As we grow closer to Jesus, some of the difficulties of earlier stages of faith disappear. We are no longer frightened by his expectation of total commitment. Smaller commitments help create the courage for greater and greater commitment. Likewise, old excuses and familiar patterns of resistance collapse as a practiced ministry cultivates a trusting attitude toward God. These changes are often imperceptible.

The disciples, who often misunderstood Jesus' vision of the kingdom, who were often confused by his teachings, ultimately stood firm in their witness to Christ's call. As the first disciples grew in their faith, so do contemporary disciples. The pattern, content, and expectation have not changed. Christ still says, "Follow me." Christ still invites believers to lovingly serve others. Christ still expects our ultimate commitment and unrestrained trust.

CLOSING WORSHIP

Locate the chorus "Lord, Prepare Me to Be a Sanctuary" in a praise hymnbook. Find a partner. Discuss how the call of Jesus to total commitment and to servanthood can help you experience the life and power of God's rule. Talk about ways you can serve others. Offer a prayer for your conversation partner in which you ask that he or she might grow in trust, commitment, and servanthood. After a time of prayer, sing, "Lord, Prepare Me to Be a Sanctuary" with the entire group.

[1]From *Growing in the Life of Faith: Education and Christian Practices,* by Craig Dykstra (Geneva Press, 1999); pages 42-43.

Session

6

COMMON COMPLICATIONS

Ruth 1; 2 Kings 5

The power, purpose, and promise of God's call in Jesus often meet our personal resistance. In this session, we will explore grief and pride, two common complications that can affect our response to God's call, and what we can learn from Ruth and Naomi's grief and Naaman's pride about the care and grace of God.

GATHERING

As you gather, list ways people run from, ignore, deny, or resist God. These may be as simple as maintaining a cynical perspective or as complex as the student who wants to understand every implication of every piece of Scripture before giving a wholehearted yes to God. Check the list: Are some of these behaviors familiar or do they remind you of yourself at another period of life? After reflection, listen to a simple and familiar hymn, such as "Softly and Tenderly Jesus is Calling," "Jesus Calls Us O'er the Tumult," or "Lord, You Have Come to the Lakeshore." Offer a prayer asking God to soften hearts and minds that all may hear and respond to God's call.

Desert Journeys

When my children were young, we planned a trip to the desert. Both daughters were fascinated by my stories of endless horizons, low scrubby trees able to survive intense heat, and dry creek beds that became roaring streams within minutes. They were ready to go until their schoolmates, who had never left the east to travel west, told them they were crazy. "There's nothing in the desert. Tell your mom to take you to Busch Gardens." I encouraged my crestfallen daughters to wait and see. I explained that the wilderness held more than any amusement park. They waited. That summer we traveled to the southwest. My children grew to love the openness of the west, and each learned a small measure of wisdom from their desert vacation.

Looking back, I acknowledge my anger at their classmates' responses. I also admit I was not completely honest with my daughters. The desert not only is a place to marvel at God's intricate creation, the desert is also a wilderness where life is difficult, heat scorches hopes, thirst dominates, and those who are wise are tempted to run back to the safety of a settled land. I knew, sooner or later, my daughters would come to know the full reality of the desert. As a parent, however, my hope was to introduce them to the wonders of desert living prior to the discovery of desert terrors.

Wilderness Witness

What other kinds of experiences might be described as wilderness experiences?

In the Bible, the wilderness suggests the journey of the Hebrews from Egypt to the Promised Land, a journey in which they endured many hardships and temptations. God led them through the wilderness, gave them the Law in the wilderness, and shaped them into the people of God in the wilderness. Elijah was sustained by God in the wilderness. Jesus encountered temptation that helped him grasp the depth of his call in the wilderness. In every case, the wilderness was the setting for survival, growth, and a willingness to respond more fully to the call of God.

People often use the word *wilderness* as a metaphor to represent times of emotional turmoil or uncertainty. Wilderness time may come through the experience of loss, such as the death of a loved one, the loss of a job, the common impact of aging, a serious injury, or illness resulting in physical limitation. Moreover, wilderness time may come through a completely different, and somewhat surprising, source: accomplishments.

Although human gifts and opportunities are given by God and intended to be used and fully developed,

> ### For Further Reflection
>
> *Kathleen Norris has written several books about life with God, with one another, and with one's self. Her collection of short pieces titled* Dakota *bears the subtitle* A Spiritual Geography. *Her words reveal the strong impact of the physical landscape, weather, and substance of South Dakota on her spirit, faith, and experience of God.*
>
> *Think about your relation to particular places and your spiritual insights. Where did you first become aware of God's presence in your life? How did the geography of that place shape your spiritual hunger, quest, and satisfaction?*

nothing we achieve, make, or accomplish replaces God. Whenever what we do becomes more important than the God who is the source of all life, we enter the wilderness of pride. Human pride is just another way of saying, "I don't need God. I can manage life on my own."

The call of God rings out in the wilderness just as in all other "places" in daily life. Perhaps you have had an experience in which you felt as though you were in a spiritual wilderness, hungering and thirsting for a sense of God's presence. Or perhaps you have walked with a brother or sister through such a spiritual wilderness. If so, you know the geography.

The Wilderness of Grief

Richard's wife, Maria, was too young to die. She was a gifted teacher and mentored many young Hispanic students whose families had moved to their community. She developed cancer; and after a brave, year-long fight, she died. Richard and the children, two grieving parents, and a school of admiring teacher colleagues and students were devastated by her loss. Richard struggled in his wilderness of grief.

73

> *How do you respond to Richard's thoughts about God? What experiences of loss have caused you or someone you know to ask similar questions? Talk about your thoughts with one or two others. Imagine that you are a friend to Richard. Drawing on your experiences with grief, consider how you could walk with him, talk with him, and support him in his grief.*

How could God take his wife? Why would God leave him to raise their children without Maria. It wasn't fair!

Perhaps you have experienced a wilderness of grief like Richard's. In such a wilderness, it is all too easy to blame God and to resist God's call to new life After a loss, God's radiant call to new life may seem like a mirage. Wandering day after day in an emotional desert increases one's sense of neediness. In the

> *Recall a wilderness of grief or loss in your life. What was this event? How did you get through the wilderness? How was God present?*

desert of mourning, one may experience too little love, too many searing memories, and too little energy for too many tasks. This is rugged terrain.

Wilderness travelers need someone, or a circle of someones, to walk alongside, to offer a shoulder of support, and to share the burden of grief. With a companion who is wise in traveling through spiritual deserts, even those in mourning, can begin to see tiny signs of hope. Small moments of kindness and support take on the subtle beauty of the desert. These signs of love refresh the spirit as an afternoon thundershower, a cactus in blossom, a lizard well adapted to his environment, a hawk circling high above, and the early morning light painting rocks and cliffs in rainbow colors. Tiny displays of hope and a wise companion turn desert traveling from terrible to tolerable.

Ruth and Naomi

The Book of Ruth offers a profound witness to God's providence to two women living in the desert of mourning. In order to survive, they must rely on one another. Throughout the story, God is with Naomi and Ruth in the wilderness of grief and desperation and provides what they need.

74

The tale opens with a grim reality. A terrible famine plagued the land of Judah. In ancient days, one solution to a famine was relocation. Families bundled their meager belongings together and began walking. Dependent on the hospitality of strangers, people traveled to new lands that might offer a chance for survival.

Elimelech and Naomi and their sons left their homeland and settled in Moab. The sons married Moabite women, Ruth and Orpah; and their marriages offered hope of another generation for their family.

However, hardship struck again: Naomi lost her husband and her two sons. Bereft of kin and security, she decided to return to her homeland to seek a relative willing to take her in. She proposed her plan to her daughters-in-law, explaining that they must return to their mothers' homes (Ruth 1:8). She could provide them with nothing. Orpah returned to her mother's home, and Ruth pledged to stay with Naomi, to share her life, to worship her God, and to die with her.

In their wilderness of grief and the desperate need to survive, Naomi and Ruth returned to Bethlehem. When old acquaintances recognized and greeted Naomi, she replied, "Call me no longer Naomi, call me Mara, for the Almighty has dealt bitterly with me. I went away full, but the LORD has brought me back empty; why call me Naomi when the LORD has dealt harshly with me, and the Almighty has brought calamity upon me?" (Ruth 1:20-21).

Read Ruth 1. Recreate the events and conversations among Ruth, Naomi, Orpah, and the acquaintances in Bethlehem. Place the events and conversations in a contemporary setting such as a train station or a homeless shelter. Present the situation of these two women as if they are caught in contemporary circumstances of dislocation, death of spouses, and financial destitution. How do you see community support at work in the story? How might community support be available for them in our contemporary culture?

The name *Naomi* means "pleasant," and the name *Mara* means bitter. Naomi blames God for her misfortune.

Yet, in spite of Naomi's bitterness and grief, God provided for them and called them to new life through the resources of a community that allowed aliens, orphans, and widows to glean the fields (Deuteronomy 24:21; Ruth 2) and through the ancient levirate law (Deuteronomy

25:5-10). Naomi refers to this law in Ruth 1:11-13.

The levirate law established a place for a widowed woman with her brother-in-law. The first son born of this union would bear her dead husband's name. Later in the story, after Ruth met Boaz and Naomi realized that he was a kinsman, she gave Ruth instructions that would lead to a marriage. Boaz made arrangements so that he could fulfill the obligations of the levirate law (4:1-6), and he married Ruth. This marriage produced a son, Obed, who, according to the women of Bethlehem, would restore Naomi's life and nourish her old age (4:13-15).

The Wilderness of Pride

Rita, an upper level manager in a major corporation, reacted with anger when her physician told her that she needed surgery. She had just initiated a complete reorganization of the corporate offices, the end-of-year reports were three weeks behind schedule, and a new manager from an ill-timed merger was stirring up trouble among the staff. It just was not time to take a few weeks off. Rita was convinced that no one else would be able to handle the situation if she were not there.

> *What evidence of pride do you see exhibited by Rita's frustration? What might help Rita trust others to do some of her work? How might the environment of the office be altered by Rita's absence?*

Pride, as all human traits, has a good and an evil face. In current usage, the word indicates a sense of one's dignity or value, self-respect, pleasure, or satisfaction in an achievement or possession, all of which are positive attitudes. When a child is developing autonomy, mastering skills and asserting self, a sense of pride or self-esteem is invaluable.

Pride, or the excessive love of one's own excellence, is also the first of the seven deadly sins (pride, covetousness, lust, envy, gluttony, anger, and sloth). It suggests being swollen with arrogance. The Bible speaks of this trait as destructive (Proverbs 16:18) and as repugnant to God (1 Peter 5:5).

Pride often indicates a distorted perception of human mastery. However, no human is able to predict and manage every event that occurs in life or every struggle in a journey through a "wilderness." All eventually meet something that cannot be managed, fixed, purchased, mastered, or dismissed. The more successful we have been in life, the easier it is to control or manage anything that comes our way. We are deluded by the more negative and sinful dimensions of pride that keep us pushing too hard and controlling too long.

> *Think of the experiences, accomplishments, and possessions that increased your sense of pride as a child. What nurtures a healthy sense of adult pride? Are there any similarities?*

Pride closes our ears to suggestions that do not build on our own accomplishments. It complicates our ability to hear the call of God and substitutes excessive trust in oneself for trust in God. It can kill our desire to know and enjoy God forever. Such pride is idolatry.

> *What are contemporary examples of idolatrous pride?*

Such a Small Thing

The story of Naomi and Ruth begins in famine and moves through grief to blessing. The story of Naaman in 2 Kings 5 begins with power and respect and moves through leprosy to humility before God. As Naomi and Ruth experienced the witness of God's steadfast love and provision through one another and through kin, so Naaman, a strong and self-reliant man, was

> *Read Naaman's story in 2 Kings 5. Review the highlights printed here. How do you see pride at work in the story? How does pride affect healing? How does Naaman overcome his pride? What connections can you make between Rita, the upper level manager in a major corporation, and Naaman?*

in need of a witness. His witness, however, did not come from a family member but from a slave girl.

In this story, one who has great power finds himself weak and unable to get the healing he wants, while one without power knows quite clearly the path to healing and hope.

Let's look at the twists of this passage noting particularly the role played by pride and self-assertion.

- A slave girl from the land of Israel (booty brought back from victory over Samaria) suggests a solution to Naaman's leprosy by telling her mistress of a prophet in her country who is able to heal (5:1-3).
- Naaman petitions his king, the king of Aram, who gives him a letter of introduction to the king of Israel that requests healing (5:4).
- Presenting this letter to the King of Israel causes the king to tear his clothes because of an apparently impossible demand to heal Naaman. The king of Israel assumes that the king of Aram is provoking an argument with him (5:5-7).
- Elisha, prophet of God, offers to heal Naaman. Elisha's goal is to witness God's great power to Naaman and his nation. The king accepts and directs Naaman to the prophet (5:8-9).
- Naaman goes to Elisha's house, but he is met by a messenger with Elisha's directions to wash himself seven times in the Jordan River and he would be healed. Outraged that there is no show, no grand gesture, and no magnificent ritual, Naaman turns his horses and chariots away (5:10-12).
- Naaman's servants reminded him of the healing he sought. Since he would have done "something difficult," why could he not complete the prophet's small assignment? Naaman lowers himself into the Jordan seven times and is healed (5:13-14).
- Naaman returns to the prophet intending to express his gratitude with gifts. Elisha, however, refuses. Naaman asks for soil in order to offer sacrifice to the God of Israel (5:15-19).

> *What small thing is God asking you to do? What keeps you from responding to God? How are you like Naaman? How are you different from him?*

Pride is not a small thing. It blocks the blessed life God offers. Naaman's pride called for the grandiose gesture rather than the apparently small act of washing his body in a river in a foreign land. The "small" people—slaves and servants—communicated God's call to healing to this mighty general. In the wilderness of Naaman's pride, and in spite of his pride, Naaman received God's healing. Thus, the prophet Elisha demonstrated the power of God and taught humility before God as the proper conduct of a blessed life.

We Are in This Together

Whether we live in the desert of mourning or on a secure mountain of self-accomplishment, one way that God's call breaks into our lives is through other people who are able to say, I understand, I'm sorry, look there, listen here, observe this, consider that. Humans are designed to live in harmony and unity with God and with one another. We are not formed to "suffer in silence" or "bear burdens alone."

> *What persons in your life have taught you, led you, walked alongside you, or witnessed to the Christian faith as a source of strength for you? Find a partner and tell one another about these people.*

Emotionally, physically, mentally, and spiritually we are formed to engage in life together. We have minds that percolate ideas and mouths that share those ideas. We have ears to listen and empathy that can motivate us to respond to human need. Because we are so designed, we are able to bring our deep spiritual experiences of God to one another as witness to the beauty, power, and love of God.

We are designed to live in community when days are pleasant and when times are difficult. We are meant to receive witness from others and to give witness to others. Frequently, this witness of giving and receiving is provoked by deprivation and frustration. For the individual wandering in the desert of mourning, a witness is a friend able to share that barren landscape and gently point out the signs of life.

For the individual proudly defending a mountain of accomplishments, a witness is a friend who knows the path to true security. A witness is like a sign pointing to God. We are in this life in faith together through times of loss and under the burden of self; together we hear, respond, and know our God.

Companion to the Weak and the Strong

God calls to the weak and to the strong, to those in the shadow of the valley of death and to those who sit in palaces wielding power. God also places witnesses near the weak and the strong. It is usually easier to offer compassion and spiritual friendship to those who are weak—to the mourning, the ill, the infirm, the depressed, and the distraught. However, it is just as important to offer correction and spiritual friendship to those who by their trust in their self-importance fail to hear God's offer of life abundant and eternal.

Our God not only calls, but also provides witnesses able to amplify the call. The experiences of grief and pride are common to all; just as common are friends who can help us to hear and respond to God's call to new life.

CLOSING WORSHIP

Sing or read the hymn "Jesus Calls Us O'er the Tumult." Prayerfully consider how you might help others hear the call of God to healing and new life. Close with The Lord's Prayer.

Additional Activities

• *Consider ways your group or your local church might offer care to those who are grieving. One program for lay pastoral ministry is Stephen Ministry. For more information about Stephen Ministries, contact Stephen Ministries at 2045 Innerbelt Business Center Dr., St. Louis, MO 63114; telephone, 314-428-2600; Web site, www.stephenministries.org.*

• *Many extended families live vast distances from each other. This situation offers new avenues for personal freedom and growth but also contains the seeds of loneliness and discouragement for those who feel separated from family. Consider ways your local church might meet the needs of such persons. Some congregations respond to this situation by promoting intergenerational programs that offer a sense of family.*

GOD'S CALL TO NEW LIFE

John 3:1-21; 4:1-42

God calls us to new life—a life that is buoyed by love and anchored in faith. To receive that life, Christians are invited to journey with Jesus in the company of others who follow him. Such response often requires change. This session sketches the invitation, response, and direction of new life through a learned Pharisee named Nicodemus and an unnamed Samaritan woman.

GATHERING

Spend a few moments thinking about unexpected changes you have experienced in your life or the lives of family members and friends. Consider the experiences of falling in love, beginning a new job, moving to a new community, or starting over again with a friendship. How have you witnessed new life emerge? How could the phrase "born again" be used to describe the experience? Light a candle and sit silently. Consider the following questions: What do I really want from God? What does God want from me? Read Psalm 51:10-17. Pray for those who long for a new heart and a right spirit.

A Call for New Life

The question "What do I really want from God?" may include a hint about our receptiveness to God's call. At times, especially in crisis, we call on God to change the circumstances of our lives: Make my dad's heart healthy, give my wife a better job, reconcile the divisions at church, change everything. The short form of those prayerful petitions is, "Grant me a new life."

At other times, perhaps more reflective times, we pray for the inner resources to handle the circumstances of our lives: Give me patience, increase my compassion, settle my restless spirit, and help me keep a focus in the midst of turmoil. The summary of those petitions might be, "Create in me a new spirit." Such praying helps us when we need new lives and a new spirit.

Often as we pray about our particular challenges and struggles, we fail to notice that God is already calling to us to accept a new spirit and to enter the new life prepared for us. Indeed, God's call makes amazing connections between one's inner spiritual life and the actual circumstances in the world. Our God is not an either/or God who either adjusts the spirit or changes the externals. Our God works tirelessly for reconciliation in every aspect of life, and God is persistent in calling individuals into new life.

> Discuss Mary Louise's circumstances. If you were faced with such change, what would be your prayer? What are some other examples of change that may be difficult but that may also hold the promise of new life? How do you see God's presence in such instances?

The setting for change, both inner and outer, may be full of both turmoil and promise. Consider this scenario: Mary Louise was happy in her position at work. As a young professional woman she was on her corporation's fast track. One day, without a previous hint, her supervisor called her into the office. After announcing how pleased the corporation was with Mary Louise's work, she was offered a new position. It was located 1,200 miles away in a community Mary Louise had never visited. Mary Louise felt a rush of joy and a pang of sadness. How could she leave her family and friends? How could she say no to such an inviting opportunity?

Walking home that night, Mary Louise stopped at a chapel to pray. She felt both fear and excitement. Change was on her horizon. Mary Louise needed and sought God's direction.

Christ Among Us

When I honestly put myself into the stories of Scripture, I wonder about my response to the call of Jesus. Perhaps your wonderings are like mine: Would I have been like the fishermen who dropped their nets and followed? Would I have been content to be among the crowd begging a miracle for my family? Would I have harshly judged Jesus by all my religious leaders told me was true? Would I have been a Pharisee trying to trap him in a legal argument or a Samaritan trying to test his credentials?

In the stories recorded in Scripture, there are those who hear God's word and do it and those who shut up their ears and keep doing what they have always done.

In this book, we have considered God's call to be God's people in a variety of ways. Often, God's call comes through ordinary conversations with others, especially with others who seek to faithfully follow Jesus. In his ministry, Jesus used a conversational approach in order to draw men and women, perhaps even children, near to him and to God.

Because this conversation continues among believers, the call of God is intricately woven into everyday experiences. As Christians share deep matters, strong hunches, and vibrant truths, God's call breaks through time and again. Through honest and faithful discussion, Christ enters circles of conversation. Where two or three are gathered together in his name, Christ is there.

As we talk about our lives, our hopes, our fears and our dreams, Jesus Christ invites us to live abundantly, hope steadfastly, dismiss fears unequivocally, and follow him.

Back to Square One

Sometimes less is truly more. In our conversations, this is frequently true. Many people talk too much and their conversation wanders too widely. Once, when I was preparing to lead a class of ministers, I became frustrated by time restraints and by all the material I thought they needed to know. God called me back through Eugene Peterson's words:

"The Christian life consists in what God does for us, not what we do for God; the Christian life consists in what God says to us, not what we say about God. We also, of course, do things and say things; but if we do not return to Square One each time we act, each time we speak, beginning from God and God's Word, we will soon be found to be practicing a spirituality that has little or nothing to do with God. . . . We need to return to Square One for a fresh start as often as every morning, noon and night"[1]

It rings true. When we fail to ground our conversation in God's word and our experience of God, it is more difficult to hear God. Although God can and does break through the cacophony of our secular lives, God's call can often be heard more easily through the spirited and faithful conversation of Christian friends. Let's look at two conversations from the Gospel of John. In each, Jesus is direct and inviting.

You Want Me to Do What?

The conversation between Jesus and Nicodemus occurred at night. We do not know why Nicodemus approached Jesus at night. Perhaps it was a safe time. It might have been that he did not want to be seen by other Pharisees or by Jesus' disciples. Whatever the reason, Nicodemus, a teacher of Israel, was a man who recognized the presence of God in the signs that Jesus was able to do.

> *Find a partner. Read John 3:1-21. Together, write a contemporary version of the conversation between Jesus and Nicodemus and present it to the group. Discuss the following questions: If you were Nicodemus, how would you approach Jesus? If you were Jesus, how would feel; or what would you think about a nighttime approach?*

In the conversation with Jesus, Nicodemus received more than he anticipated and, apparently, more than he could comprehend. After he finished affirming Jesus as a holy and Godly teacher, Jesus responded with a new teaching. "Very truly, I tell you, no one can see the kingdom of God without being born from above" (John 3:3). Jesus, aptly attuning himself to the subtext of Nicodemus's words, directed the nighttime seeker toward God and especially toward God's season of salvation, a season initiated by none other that Jesus.

With well-chosen words, Jesus announced that Nicodemus must be born again. The Greek word *anōthen* is translated "again" in the King James Version and the New InternationalVersion of the Bible and "from above" in the New Revised Standard Version. The Greek word suggests a range of meanings: from above, from the first, anew, again, and from the top.

The word that is translated "born" also suggests "regenerate," "make," and "conceive." These well-chosen words opened the space for Nicodemus to catch a vision of God's kingdom and to glimpse himself within that vision. The phrase "born from above" (spoken by Jesus in Aramaic and offered by John's Gospel in Greek) held three different nuances: Born again, a temporal connotation for physical birth; born anew, a personal description of inner change; and born from above, a spiritual nuance of divine intervention.

Read John 3:3 aloud. Which nuance of meaning means most to you: born again, born anew, or born from above? Explain your response. In what ways, if any, have the phrases "born again," "born anew," or "born from above" been problematic for you, your congregation, or your community? What possibilities for new life do you see in these phrases?

Nicodemus faced an interpretive challenge. As the conversation moved forward, it was clear that Nicodemus accepted the temporal connotation of Jesus' words. Nicodemus protested that no one could reenter a mother's womb; birth is a one-time event. Jesus responds to Nicodemus's literal understanding with another level of meaning: "Very truly, I tell you, no one can enter the kingdom of God without being born of water and Spirit. What is born of the flesh is flesh, and what is born of the Spirit is spirit. Do not be astonished that I said to you, 'You must be born from above' " (John 3:5-7).

Nicodemus remains perplexed. Jesus continues with a longer speech in which he notes the failure to receive testimony. "If I have told you about earthly things and you do not believe, how can you believe if I tell you about heavenly things?" (John 3:12). He continues with more teaching about the Son of Man, God's gift of life in the Son, and belief in the Son of God.

We do not know from Scripture if Nicodemus fully grasped Jesus' words. In John 7:50, Nicodemus points to Jewish law when he says to the chief priests and other Pharisees, "Our law does not judge people without first giving them a hearing to find out what they are doing, does it?" John 19:39 tells us that he assisted Joseph of Arimathea with the burial of Jesus' body according to Jewish custom. We can, however, imagine that he receded into the night pondering Jesus' words and the call to rebirth.

Yet this conversation offers Nicodemus and all who read about it an opportunity to glimpse new life in God's kingdom. Nicodemus pondered in the dark, "How can these things be?"

There's That Good News Again

Nicodemus met Jesus under the cover of darkness, the Samaritan woman found Jesus by Jacob's well in the heat and light of midday. These two conversations, recorded in the Gospel of John, are as unlike in staging, style, and content as any conversations recorded chapter to chapter in the Bible.

Read John 4:1-42. Join with other participants in your group to reenact this event. Assume the roles of the woman, Jesus, the disciples, and the other Samaritans who believe Jesus. Present the reading to the group. With which of the characters do you most identify? least identify? why? What does this passage say to you about issues related to gender? to religious prejudice? What does it say to you about Jesus?

In the first conversation, a faithful Jewish leader approached a faithful Jewish teacher, man-to-man and piously correct. In the second conversation, Jesus crossed a boundary into Samaria and is, indeed, crossing a social boundary by directly requesting a drink from a Samaritan woman.

Jews and Samaritans had a history of enmity, and the relationship between these two groups was marked by prejudice on both sides. The style of the second conversation is also different. In the first conversation, Nicodemus has little to offer to the conversation other than his inability to grasp the phrase "born from above." Jesus and the Samaritan woman have a more balanced dialogue. She says more. When Jesus asks her for a drink of water, she expresses her surprise by responding, "How is it that you, a Jew, ask a drink of me, a woman of Samaria?" Jesus shifts to a spiritual level of meaning with a response about the gift of God, his identity, and living water.

The Samaritan woman continues to engage Jesus in conversation about water. She speaks in terms of the literal connections to "living water" while Jesus' remarks use spiritually charged metaphors and images. Eventually, the two exchange places. In the second half of the conversation, Jesus engages the woman in conversation about her practical life, and she responds from her spiritual resources with remarks about the differences in worship between Jews and Samaritans and about her belief in the coming Messiah.

This part of their conversation contains Jesus' self-affirmation as the Messiah. The conversation with the woman at the well is marked by length, a sense of banter between Jesus and the Samaritan woman, a definition of true worship, and Jesus' disclosure of his identity. All these elements weave together to produce a unique call to an unlikely follower.

The consequence of Jesus' call to the woman at the well was her recognition, similar to Nicodemus' recognition, that Jesus was certainly a prophet. The Samaritan woman goes one step further when she suggests that he might be the Messiah. She told people about her encounter. They in turn, invited Jesus to remain with them, and many Samaritans believed in him. Subsequently, they told the woman, "It is no longer because of what you said that we believe, for we have heard for ourselves, and we know that this is truly the Savior of the world" (John 4:41-42).

Because of her conversation with Jesus in bright daylight beside Jacob's Well, the Samaritan woman delivered a bold invitation to all who would listen to her, "Come and see a man who told me everything I have ever done. He cannot be the Messiah, can he?" (John 4:29). As a result, other Samaritans listened to him and believed.

Change flowed from the Samaritan woman's conversation with Jesus, but this story changed more than the life of one woman and more than the life of one community. This conversation, open and questioning, changed the boundary line between God's chosen people and all others and illuminated the inclusive ministry of Jesus. He would not and will not be limited by social, religious, ethnic, racial, or any condition of human life. On God's behalf, Jesus calls all to new life. No boundary lines remain in place once Jesus begins a conversation.

Possibility and Hope

The story of Nicodemus and of the Samaritan woman provide a context for learning about the content of God's call to new life: conversation. Nicodemus struggled to understand Jesus' words. The Samaritan woman struggled with the conversation about water, but she was amazed by Jesus' ability to see what her life was like. Her amazement led her to tell others about her experience with Jesus and to question whether or not he might be the Messiah.

Every call begins with an attentive individual who listens to God in the good and bad circumstances of everyday life. We may have to overcome our own misunderstanding, our own struggles, and our own amazement in order to fully hear and comprehend God's call to new life. Like Mary Louise in the beginning of this session, we may have to overcome fear in order to make a life choice. Whether Mary Louise takes the job offer or remains near her family and friends, God promises new life.

God's call is simultaneously attractive, providential, surprising, and transforming in every life circumstance. Whether we comprehend slowly or swiftly, whether we must overcome misunderstanding or amazement, God's call in Jesus always contains possibility and hope.

CLOSING WORSHIP

Praying with God's gift of imagination gives form and shape to religious intuition. The following prayer exercise is designed to lead you into a conversation with Jesus:

Sit in a comfortable position. Become quiet by focusing your attention on your breathing. Be open to God's presence. When you are relaxed, imagine your dinner table, complete with family or friends. Using your mind's eye, look carefully at the surroundings. Imagine that one empty place exists at your table. As you enjoy a meal with loved ones, Jesus enters the room. He joins the company at your table and greets everyone. Jesus is completely at ease in your home, at your table, and among your family and friends. Listen, now to all that Jesus says to your diners as a group and to each individually. Listen with particular attention to what Jesus says to you. After Jesus says "Peace, farewell." Gradually return your thoughts and awareness to your actual location. Offer a prayer of gratitude for any insights you have gained by using your imagination to pray. Close the session by singing a hymn, such as "Softly and Tenderly Jesus is Calling" or "Lord, You Have Come to the Lakeshore."

[1]From *Subversive Spirituality*, by Eugene H. Peterson (William B. Eerdmans Publishing Company, 1997); pages 30-31.

Appendix

Background Scriptures for "Call: Called to Be God's People"

Genesis 11:27–12:9
1 Samuel 16:1-4b
("to meet him"), 6-13;
2 Samuel 7:8-16
Matthew 1
Luke 2:22-38
Mark 1:14-28
Mark 2:13-17

Mark 6:6b-13
(start with "Then he"); 3:13-19
Mark 8:27-38
Mark 10:13-45
Ruth 1
2 Kings 5
John 3:1-21
John 4:1-42

The Committee on the Uniform Series

The Committee on the Uniform Series (CUS) is made up of persons appointed by their respective denominations, which, although differing in certain elements of faith and polity, hold a common faith in Jesus Christ, the Son of God, as Lord and Savior, whose saving gospel is to be taught to all humankind.

CUS has about 70 members who represent nineteen protestant denominations in the US and Canada, who work together to develop the International Bible Lessons for Christian Teaching. A team from this committee develops the cycles of Scriptures and themes that form the backbone of the Bible lesson development guides. The cycles present a balance between Old and New Testaments, although the weight is on the latter. Cycles through 2016 are organized around the following themes: Creation, call, covenant, Christ, community, commitment, God, hope, worship, tradition, faith, and justice.

—MARVIN CROPSEY,
Chair, Committee on the Uniform Series

Other Bible Study Resources

If your group would like to study other short-term small-group resources, we suggest the following:

The Jesus Collection. A series of books about the life, teachings, and ministry of Jesus Christ, each of which invites the reader into renewal and commitment.

The Life and Letters of Paul Series. Historical, archaeological, and geographic data interwoven into a fascinating study of Paul's epistles. Each book takes an in-depth look at particular aspects of Paul's ministry as illuminated in his letters.

The FaithQuestions Series. Offers studies of issues in theology, ethics, missions, biblical interpretation, and church history. Designed for adults who seek a deeper engagement with the Christian faith and with Scripture.

If your group would like to explore a long-term Bible study, we recommend:

Adult Bible Study. Published quarterly. Thirteen lessons per quarter. Bible study resources based on the International Lesson Series, also known as the Uniform Series.

Genesis to Revelation. A comprehensive study based on the New International Version of the Bible. Twenty-four volumes. Thirteen sessions per volume.

Journey Through the Bible. A comprehensive study based on the New Revised Standard Version of the Bible. Sixteen Volumes. Thirteen sessions per volume.

DISCIPLE Bible Study. A 34-week foundation study of the Bible in which participants learn how to become more effective disciples through Bible study.